The Living Word for Living Life

God's Path to Success in Every Situation

The Living Word for Living Life: God's Path to Success in Every Situation

© 2010 by Vanable H. Moody II

Please visit us at:

www.vanmoody.org or www.theworshipcentercc.org

Printed in the United States of America

1 2 3 4 5 6 7   10 11 12 13 14 15 16

ISBN: 978-0-9844636-0-2

Acknowledgments

To my wife, Dr. Ty: Your constant love and faith encourages me to keep dreaming.

To my kids, Eden Sydney & Ethan Isaiah: Every day I thank God for allowing you to be in my life.

To Beth Clark: We make a great team. I look forward to all God wants us to accomplish for His glory!

Contents

Section I
The Living Word for Living Life in Your Relationships................ 1

Section 2
The Living Word for Living Life When You Need Hope 17

Section 3
The Living Word for Living Life When You Need Wisdom in Practical Matters...41

Section 4

The Living Word for Living Life While You're Waiting for Your Breakthrough

Section 5

The Living Word for Living Life When You're Struggling with Negative Emotions and Experiences

Section 6

The Living Word for Living Life When You Feel Vulnerable or Alone

Section 7

The Living Word for Living Life with God

Section 8

The Living Word for Living Life When You Want to Celebrate ... 107

Topics in Alphabetical Order

The Living Word for Living Life

Quick Reference Guide to Stressful Situations and Crises*

*All of this is in cooperation with, not in exclusion of, the ministry of healing of medical science. God heals in many ways and medical science is one of them. The task of this book is to put people in touch with the Master and to affirm the many ways He heals today. In the event of a medical or emotional emergency, please seek professional attention.

Introduction

$\mathcal{T}$he world is full of questions, issues, and challenges. There is only one answer to all these situations—and His name is Jesus. He is our constant companion on life's journey, and He will always lead us in triumph.

My great desire as a pastor is for people to live in victory, and the key to a victorious life is the ability to speak the Word of God over every situation. Proverbs 18:21 declares: "Death and life are in the power of the tongue." This means that when we speak God's Word, we bring life, hope, freedom, wisdom, success and power into the circumstances of our everyday lives. Isaiah 55:11 promises that His Word will not return void; it will not fail to accomplish its purpose. Knowing God's Word in our hearts and speaking it with our mouths brings change to our situations, even the ones that seem impossible. We don't have to live in weakness, confusion or defeat. We can overcome by the Word of God!

The power to live life today cannot be found in our own strength or in the world's resources; it only exists in the Word of the Lord. Jesus said in John 6:63: "The flesh profits nothing. The words that I speak to you are spirit, and they are life." God's Word offers divine insight and perfect advice for any issue or challenge life presents. More than we need to know what other people—even so-called experts—say about the situations that affect us, we need to know what God says.

But God says a lot! His Word is packed with wisdom on a vast variety of topics, and sometimes we find ourselves flipping through the pages of our Bibles looking for certain verses when what we really need is to be able to quickly access His Word for our specific circumstances. This is the reason I have put together *The Living Word for Living Life*. I want you to be able to look up a situation you're facing and be able to get God's Word on it immediately.

This book is designed as tool you can use to find what you need from God as soon as you need it. Here are a few ways to make this book most effective in your life:

Familiarize yourself with the **table of contents.** It's arranged so you can glance at the general section headings and then easily see the specific topical areas in which you need God's truth and power.

Get acquainted with the subjects this book addresses by taking a look at the **alphabetical list of topics** and perhaps even putting a mark next to the ones that most apply to your life.

If you find yourself in a crisis or stressful situation, go to the page entitled, **"Quick Reference Guide to Stressful Situations and Crises."** It will not only point you to Bible verses and passages that can help you, it will also encourage you to seek the practical support or assistance you may need in an emergency.

For an expanded list of the many subject this book covers and to further encourage yourself by learning scriptures on related topics, turn to the back of the book and look through the expanded index, entitled **"Where to Find It."**

Nothing you can ever do in life will help you as much as knowing God's Word, believing it in your heart and speaking it from your mouth. You are well on your way to a life of victory and greatness. This book will help you get there—and I bless you on your journey!

—Van Moody

Section 1

The Living Word for Living Life in Your Relationships

Children

Family

Marriage

Enemies

Children

*D*on't you see that children are God's best gift? the fruit of the womb his generous legacy? Like a warrior's fistful of arrows are the children of a vigorous youth.

Oh, how blessed are you parents, with your quivers full of children! Your enemies don't stand a chance against you; you'll sweep them right off your doorstep.

PSALM 127:3-5, MSG

Train up a child in the way he should go [and in keeping with his individual gift or bent], and when he is old he will not depart from it.

PROVERBS 22:6, AMP

Young people are prone to foolishness and fads; the cure comes through tough-minded discipline.

PROVERBS 22:15, MSG

The rod and reproof give wisdom, but a child who gets his own way brings shame to his mother.

PROVERBS 29:15, NASB

At that time Jesus said, "I praise you, Father, Lord of heaven and earth, because you have hidden these things from the wise and learned, and revealed them to little children.

MATTHEW 11:25, NIV

So they said, "Believe on the Lord Jesus Christ, and you will be saved, you and your household."

ACTS 16:31, NKJV

"For the promise is to you and to your children, and to all who are afar off, as many as the Lord our God will call."

ACTS 2:39, NKJV

All your children will be taught by the Lord, and your children will have unlimited peace.

ISAIAH 54:13, GOD'S WORD

The disciples shooed them off. But Jesus was irate and let them know it: "Don't push these children away. Don't ever get between them and me. These children are at the very center of life in the kingdom. Mark this: Unless you accept God's kingdom in the simplicity of a child, you'll never get in." Then, gathering the children up in his arms, he laid his hands of blessing on them.

MARK 10:14-16, MSG

Children's children are the crown of old men; and the glory of children are their fathers.

PROVERBS 17:6, KJV

From the lips of children and infants you have ordained praise because of your enemies, to silence the foe and the avenger.

PSALM 8:2, NIV

But the love of the Lord remains forever with those who fear him. His salvation extends to the children's children.

PSALM 103:17, NLT

Even a child is known by his acts, whether [or not] what he does is pure and right.

PROVERBS 20:11, AMP

Children, obey your parents in the Lord, for this is right. Fathers, do not provoke your children to anger, but bring them up in the discipline and instruction of the Lord.

EPHESIANS 6:1, 4, NASB

I have been young and now I am old, yet I have not seen the righteous forsaken or his descendants begging bread. All day long he is gracious and lends, and his descendants are a blessing.

PSALM 37:25, 26, NASB

He will bring justice to the poor of the people; He will save the children of the needy, and will break in pieces the oppressor.

PSALM 72:4, NKJV

We will not conceal them from their children, but tell to the generation to come the praises of the Lord, and His strength and His wondrous works that He has done. For He established a testimony in Jacob and appointed a law in Israel, which He commanded our fathers that they should teach them to their children, that the generation to come might know, even the children yet to be born, that they may arise and tell them to their children.

PSALM 78:4-6, NASB

The children of Your servants will continue, and their descendants will be established before You.

PSALM 102:28, NKJV

He grants the barren woman a home, like a joyful mother of children. Praise the Lord!

PSALM 113:9, NKJV

A good man leaves an inheritance to his children's children, and the wealth of the sinner is stored up for the righteous.

PROVERBS 13:22, NASB

In the fear of the Lord is strong confidence: and his children shall have a place of refuge.

PROVERBS 14:26, KJV

A righteous man who walks in his integrity—how blessed are his sons after him.

PROVERBS 20:7, NASB

Don't be afraid to correct your young ones; a spanking won't kill them.

PROVERBS 23:13, MSG

Family

So they said, "Believe on the Lord Jesus Christ, and you will be saved, you and your household."

ACTS 16:31, NKJV

"But if you refuse to serve the Lord, then choose today whom you will serve. Would you prefer the gods your ancestors served beyond the Euphrates? Or will it be the gods of the Amorites in whose land you now live? But as for me and my family, we will serve the Lord."

The Living Word for Living Life

Joshua 24:15, NLT

Make a clean break with all cutting, backbiting, profane talk. Be gentle with one another, sensitive. Forgive one another as quickly and thoroughly as God in Christ forgave you.

Ephesians 4:31, 32, MSG

Point your kids in the right direction—when they're old they won't be lost.

Proverbs 22:6, MSG

Honor your father and your mother, that your days may be long upon the land which the Lord your God is giving you.

Exodus 20:12, NKJV

Fathers, do not provoke your children to anger, but bring them up in the discipline and instruction of the Lord.

Ephesians 6:4, NASB

He must manage his own family well and see that his children obey him with proper respect. (If anyone does not know how to manage his own family, how can he take care of God's church?)

1 Timothy 3:4, 5, NIV

Don't you see that children are God's best gift? the fruit of the womb his generous legacy? Like a warrior's fistful of arrows are the children of a vigorous youth. Oh, how blessed are you parents, with your quivers full of children! Your enemies don't stand a chance against you; you'll sweep them right off your doorstep.

Psalm 127:3-5, MSG

Children, obey your parents in the Lord, for this is

right. Honor your father and mother (which is the first commandment with a promise), so that it may be well with you, and that you may live long on the earth.

EPHESIANS 6:1-3, NASB

"He will restore the hearts of the fathers to their children and the hearts of the children to their fathers, so that I will not come and smite the land with a curse."

MALACHI 4:6, NASB

Children's children are the crown of old men; and the glory of children are their fathers.

PROVERBS 17:6, KJV

Write these commandments that I've given you today on your hearts. Get them inside of you and then get them inside your children. Talk about them wherever you are, sitting at home or walking in the street; talk about them from the time you get up in the morning to when you fall into bed at night. Tie them on your hands and foreheads as a reminder; inscribe them on the doorposts of your homes and on your city gates.

DEUTERONOMY 6:6-9, MSG

Discipline your son, and he will give you peace; he will bring delight to your soul.

PROVERBS 29:17, NIV

A good man leaves an inheritance to his children's children, and the wealth of the sinner is stored up for the righteous.

PROVERBS 13:22, NASB

How joyful are those who fear the Lord—all who follow his ways! You will enjoy the fruit of your labor. How joyful and prosperous you will be! Your wife will be like a fruitful grapevine, flourishing within your home. Your children will be like vigorous young olive trees as they sit around your table. That is the Lord's blessing for those who fear him.

PSALM 128:1-4, NLT

The father of the [uncompromisingly] righteous (the upright, in right standing with God) shall greatly rejoice, and he who becomes the father of a wise child shall have joy in him.

PROVERBS 23:24, AMP

All your children will be taught by the Lord, and your children will have unlimited peace.

ISAIAH 54:13, GOD'S WORD

Marriage

The Lord God said, "It is not good for the man to be alone. I will make a helper suitable for him."

GENESIS 2:18, NIV

Therefore a man shall leave his father and his mother and shall become united and cleave to his wife, and they shall become one flesh.

GENESIS 2:24, AMP

"But if you refuse to serve the Lord, then choose today whom you will serve. Would you prefer the gods your ancestors served beyond the Euphrates? Or will it be the gods of the Amorites in whose land you now live? But as for me and my family, we will serve the Lord."

JOSHUA 24:15, NLT

I will behave myself wisely and give heed to the blameless way—O when will You come to me? I will walk within my house in integrity and with a blameless heart.

PSALM 101:2, AMP

Trust in the Lord with all your heart; do not depend on your own understanding. Seek his will in all you do, and he will show you which path to take.

PROVERBS 3:5, 6, NLT

Hate starts quarrels, but love covers every wrong.

PROVERBS 10:12, GOD'S WORD

Love never does anything that is harmful to a neighbor. Therefore, love fulfills Moses' Teachings.

ROMANS 13:10, GOD'S WORD

Make a clean break with all cutting, backbiting, profane talk. Be gentle with one another, sensitive. Forgive one another as quickly and thoroughly as God in Christ forgave you.

EPHESIANS 4:31, 32, MSG

Out of respect for Christ, be courteously reverent to one another. Wives, understand and support your husbands in ways that show your support for Christ. The husband provides leadership to his wife the way Christ does to his church, not by domineering but by cherishing. So just as the church submits to Christ as he exercises such leadership, wives should likewise submit to their husbands. Husbands, go all out in your love for your wives, exactly as Christ did for the church—a love marked by giving, not getting. Christ's love makes the church whole. His words evoke her beauty. Everything he does and says is designed to bring the best out of her, dressing her in dazzling white silk, radiant with holiness. And that is how husbands ought to love their wives. They're really doing themselves a favor—since they're already "one" in marriage. No one abuses his own body, does he? No, he feeds and pampers it. That's how Christ treats us, the church, since we are part of his body. And this is why a man leaves father and mother and cherishes his wife. No longer two, they become "one flesh." This is a huge mystery, and I don't pretend to understand it all. What is clearest to me is the way Christ treats the church. And this provides a good picture of how each husband is to treat his wife, loving himself in loving her, and how each wife is to honor her husband.

EPHESIANS 5:21-33, MSG

You were cleansed from your sins when you obeyed the truth, so now you must show sincere love to each other as brothers and sisters. Love each other deeply with all your heart.

1 PETER 1:22, NLT

The same goes for you wives: Be good wives to your husbands, responsive to their needs. There are husbands who, indifferent as they are to any words about God, will be captivated by your life of holy beauty. What matters is not your outer appearance—the styling of your hair, the jewelry you wear, the cut of your clothes— but your inner disposition. Cultivate inner beauty, the gentle, gracious kind that God delights in. The holy women of old were beautiful before God that way, and were good, loyal wives to their husbands. Sarah, for instance, taking care of Abraham, would address him as "my dear husband." You'll be true daughters of Sarah if you do the same, unanxious and unintimidated. The same goes for you husbands: Be good husbands to your wives. Honor them, delight in them. As women they lack some of your advantages. But in the new life of God's grace, you're equals. Treat your wives, then, as equals so your prayers don't run aground.

1 PETER 3:1-7, MSG

Summing up: Be agreeable, be sympathetic, be loving, be compassionate, be humble. That goes for all of you, no exceptions. No retaliation. No sharp-tongued sarcasm. Instead, bless—that's your job, to bless. You'll be a blessing and also get a blessing. Whoever wants to embrace life and see the day fill up with good, here's what you do: Say nothing evil or hurtful; snub evil and cultivate good; run after peace for all you're worth.

1 PETER 3:8-11, MSG

A wife of noble character is her husband's crown, but a disgraceful wife is like decay in his bones.

PROVERBS 12:4, NIV

He who finds a wife finds what is good and receives favor from the Lord.

PROVERBS 18:22, NIV

A foolish son is his father's ruin, and a quarrelsome wife is like a constant dripping.

PROVERBS 19:13, NIV

Houses and wealth are inherited from parents, but a prudent wife is from the Lord.

PROVERBS 19:14, NIV

Better to live on a corner of the roof than share a house with a quarrelsome wife.

PROVERBS 21:9, NIV

A quarrelsome wife is like a constant dripping on a rainy day.

PROVERBS 27:15, NIV

A wife of noble character who can find? She is worth far more than rubies.

PROVERBS 31:10, NIV

Enjoy life with your wife, whom you love, all the days of this meaningless life that God has given you under the sun—all your meaningless days. For this is your lot in life and in your toilsome labor under the sun.

ECCLESIASTES 9:9, NIV

To the married I give this command (not I, but the Lord): A wife must not separate from her husband.

1 CORINTHIANS 7:10, NIV

To the rest I say this (I, not the Lord): If any brother has a wife who is not a believer and she is willing to live with him, he must not divorce her.

1 CORINTHIANS 7:12, NIV

Marriage should be honored by all, and the marriage bed kept pure, for God will judge the adulterer and all the sexually immoral.

HEBREWS 13:4, NIV

Enemies

The Lord helps them and delivers them; he delivers them from the wicked and saves them, because they take refuge in him.

PSALM 37:40, NIV

Those who hate you will be clothed with shame, and the tents of the wicked shall be no more.

JOB 8:22, AMP

"The Lord shall cause your enemies who rise up against you to be defeated before you; they will come out against you one way and will flee before you seven ways."

DEUTERONOMY 28:7, NASB

For the Lord your God is the one who goes with you to fight for you against your enemies to give you victory.

DEUTERONOMY 20:4, NIV

In famine He will redeem you from death, and in war from the power of the sword.

JOB 5:20, NASB

"No weapon that is formed against you will prosper; and every tongue that accuses you in judgment you will condemn. This is the heritage of the servants of the Lord, and their vindication is from Me," declares the Lord.

ISAIAH 54:17, NASB

The Lord is on my side and takes my part, He is among those who help me; therefore shall I see my desire established upon those who hate me.

PSALM 118:7, AMP

To grant us that we, being delivered from the hand of our foes, might serve Him fearlessly.

LUKE 1:74, AMP

A wicked ruler will not be allowed to govern the land set aside for righteous people. That is why righteous people do not use their power to do wrong.

PSALM 125:3, GOD'S WORD

For in the day of trouble He will hide me in His shelter; in the secret place of His tent will He hide me; He will set me high upon a rock. And now shall my head be lifted up above my enemies round about me; in His tent I will offer sacrifices and shouting of joy; I will sing, yes, I will sing praises to the Lord.

PSALM 27:5, 6, AMP

When a man's ways please the Lord, He makes even his enemies to be at peace with him.

PROVERBS 16:7, NKJV

His heart is steady, and he is not afraid. In the end he will look triumphantly at his enemies.

PSALM 112:8, GOD'S WORD

"And will not God bring about justice for his chosen ones, who cry out to him day and night? Will he keep putting them off?"

LUKE 18:7, NIV

Behold, they may gather together and stir up strife, but it is not from Me. Whoever stirs up strife against you shall fall and surrender to you.

ISAIAH 54:15, AMP

God loves all who hate evil, and those who love him he keeps safe, snatches them from the grip of the wicked.

PSALM 97:10, MSG

"But I will deliver you in that day," says the Lord, "and you shall not be given into the hand of the men of whom you are afraid."

JEREMIAH 39:17, 18, NKJV

You must worship only the Lord your God. He is the one who will rescue you from all your enemies.

2 KINGS 17:39, NLT

So he answered, "Do not fear, for those who are with us are more than those who are with them."

2 KINGS 6:16, NKJV

Be not afraid of sudden terror and panic, nor of the stormy blast or the storm and ruin of the wicked when it comes [for you will be guiltless], for the Lord shall be your confidence, firm and strong, and shall keep your foot from being caught [in a trap or some hidden danger].

PROVERBS 3:25, 26, AMP

"Everyone who is angry with you will be ashamed and disgraced. Those who oppose you will be reduced to nothing and disappear. You will search for your enemies, but you will not find them. Those who are at war with you will be reduced to nothing and no longer exist."

ISAIAH 41:11, 12, GOD'S WORD

That we should be saved from our enemies, and from the hand of all that hate us.

LUKE 1:71, KJV

So that we may boldly say, The Lord is my helper, and I will not fear what man shall do unto me.

HEBREWS 13:6, KJV

Section 2

The Living Word for Living Life When You Need Hope

Addiction

Depression

Grief

Overcoming Difficulty

Sickness

Suffering

Temptation

Addiction

From now on, think of it this way: Sin speaks a dead language that means nothing to you; God speaks your mother tongue, and you hang on every word. You are dead to sin and alive to God. That's what Jesus did. That means you must not give sin a vote in the way you conduct your lives. Don't give it the time of day. Don't even run little errands that are connected with that old way of life. Throw yourselves wholeheartedly and full-time—remember, you've been raised from the dead!—into God's way of doing things. Sin can't tell you how to live. After all, you're not living under that old tyranny any longer. You're living in the freedom of God.

ROMANS 6:11-14, MSG

Therefore, confess your sins to one another, and pray for one another so that you may be healed. The effective prayer of a righteous man can accomplish much.

JAMES 5:16, NASB

Stand fast therefore in the liberty by which Christ has made us free, and do not be entangled again with a yoke of bondage.

GALATIANS 5:1, NKJV

But I say, walk and live [habitually] in the [Holy] Spirit [responsive to and controlled and guided by the Spirit]; then you will certainly not gratify the cravings and desires of the flesh (of human nature without God). For the desires of the flesh are opposed to the [Holy] Spirit, and the [desires of the] Spirit are opposed to the flesh (godless human nature); for these are antagonistic to each other [continually withstanding and in conflict with each other], so that you are not free but are prevented from doing what you desire to do.

GALATIANS 5:16, 17, AMP

And those who are Christ's have crucified the flesh with its passions and desires. If we live in the Spirit, let us also walk in the Spirit.

GALATIANS 5:24, 25, NKJV

For the law of the Spirit of life in Christ Jesus has set you free from the law of sin and of death.

ROMANS 8:2, NASB

Those who live according to the sinful nature have their minds set on what that nature desires; but those who live in accordance with the Spirit have their minds set on what the Spirit desires. The mind of the sinful man is death, but the mind controlled by the Spirit is life and peace; the sinful mind is hostile to God. It does not submit to God's law, nor can it do so. Those controlled by the sinful nature cannot please God. You, however, are controlled not by the sinful nature but by the Spirit, if the Spirit of God lives in you.

ROMANS 8:5-9, NIV

If then you were raised with Christ, seek those things which are above, where Christ is, sitting at the right hand of God. Set your mind on things above, not on things on the earth. For you died, and your life is hidden with Christ in God.

COLOSSIANS 3:1-3, NKJV

Do not love this world nor the things it offers you, for when you love the world, you do not have the love of the Father in you. For the world offers only a craving for physical pleasure, a craving for everything we see, and pride in our achievements and possessions. These are not from the Father, but are from this world. And this world is fading away, along with everything that people crave. But anyone who does what pleases God will live forever.

1 JOHN 2:15-17, NLT

For whatever is born of God is victorious over the world; and this is the victory that conquers the world, even our faith. Who is it that is victorious over [that conquers] the world but he who believes that Jesus is the Son of God [who adheres to, trusts in, and relies on that fact]?

1 JOHN 5:4, 5, AMP

You are of God, little children, and have overcome them, because He who is in you is greater than he who is in the world.

1 JOHN 4:4, NKJV

Be anxious for nothing, but in everything by prayer and supplication with thanksgiving let your requests be made known to God. And the peace of God, which surpasses all comprehension, will guard your hearts and your minds in Christ Jesus.

PHILIPPIANS 4:6, 7, NASB

Summing it all up, friends, I'd say you'll do best by filling your minds and meditating on things true, noble, reputable, authentic, compelling, gracious—the best, not the worst; the beautiful, not the ugly; things to praise, not things to curse. Put into practice what you learned from me, what you heard and saw and realized. Do that, and God, who makes everything work together, will work you into his most excellent harmonies.

PHILIPPIANS 4:8, 9, MSG

I can do all things through Christ who strengthens me.

PHILIPPIANS 4:13, NKJV

Submit yourselves therefore to God. Resist the devil, and he will flee from you.

JAMES 4:7, KJV

Depression

And Nehemiah continued, "Go and celebrate with a feast of rich foods and sweet drinks, and share gifts of food with people who have nothing prepared. This is a sacred day before our Lord. Don't be dejected and sad, for the joy of the Lord is your strength!"

NEHEMIAH 8:10, NLT

For His anger is but for a moment, His favor is for life; weeping may endure for a night, but joy comes in the morning.

PSALM 30:5, NKJV

The righteous cry out, and the Lord hears them; he delivers them from all their troubles.

PSALM 34:17, NIV

He heals the brokenhearted and bandages their wounds.

PSALM 147:3, NLT

But those who hope in the Lord will renew their strength. They will soar on wings like eagles; they will run and not grow weary, they will walk and not be faint.

ISAIAH 40:31, NIV

"Don't be afraid, because I am with you. Don't be intimidated; I am your God. I will strengthen you. I will help you. I will support you with my victorious right hand."

ISAIAH 41:10, GOD'S WORD

When you pass through the waters, I will be with you; and when you pass through the rivers, they will not sweep over you. When you walk through the fire, you will not be burned; the flames will not set you ablaze.

ISAIAH 43:2, NIV

The ransomed of the Lord will return. They will enter Zion with singing; everlasting joy will crown their heads. Gladness and joy will overtake them, and sorrow and sighing will flee away.

ISAIAH 51:11, NIV

To all who mourn in Israel, he will give a crown of beauty for ashes, a joyous blessing instead of mourning, festive praise instead of despair. In their righteousness, they will be like great oaks that the Lord has planted for his own glory.

ISAIAH 61:3, NLT

Jesus used this illustration with his disciples to show them that they need to pray all the time and never give up.

LUKE 18:1, GOD'S WORD

I'm absolutely convinced that nothing—nothing living or dead, angelic or demonic, today or tomorrow, high or low, thinkable or unthinkable—absolutely *nothing* can get between us and God's love because of the way that Jesus our Master has embraced us.

ROMANS 8:38, 39, MSG

Blessed be the God and Father of our Lord Jesus Christ, the Father of mercies and God of all comfort, who comforts us in all our affliction so that we will be able to comfort those who are in any affliction with the comfort with which we ourselves are comforted by God.

2 CORINTHIANS 1:3, 4, NASB

Summing it all up, friends, I'd say you'll do best by filling your minds and meditating on things true, noble, reputable, authentic, compelling, gracious—the best, not the worst; the beautiful, not the ugly; things to praise, not things to curse.

PHILIPPIANS 4:8, MSG

Dear friends, do not be surprised at the painful trial you are suffering, as though something strange were happening to you. But rejoice that you participate in the sufferings of Christ, so that you may be overjoyed when his glory is revealed.

1 PETER 4:12, 13, NIV

Humble yourselves, therefore, under God's mighty hand, that he may lift you up in due time. Cast all your anxiety on him because he cares for you.

1 PETER 5:6, 7, NIV

Grief

Even though I walk through the valley of the shadow of death, I will fear no evil, for you are with me; your rod and your staff, they comfort me.

PSALM 23:4, NIV

This is my comfort in my affliction, that Your word has revived me.

PSALM 119:50, NASB

"Don't be afraid, because I am with you. Don't be intimidated; I am your God. I will strengthen you. I will help you. I will support you with my victorious right hand."

ISAIAH 41:10, GOD'S WORD

"When you pass through the waters, I will be with you; and through the rivers, they will not overflow you. When you walk through the fire, you will not be scorched, nor will the flame burn you."

ISAIAH 43:2, NASB

"For the Lord comforts his people and will have compassion on his afflicted ones."

ISAIAH 49:13, NIV

[The Lord God says] And the redeemed of the Lord shall return and come with singing to Zion; everlasting joy shall be upon their heads. They shall obtain joy and gladness, and sorrow and sighing shall flee away.

ISAIAH 51:11, AMP

"Blessed are those who mourn, for they will be comforted."

MATTHEW 5:4, NIV

"O death, where is your victory? O death, where is your sting?" For sin is the sting that results in death, and the law gives sin its power. But thank God! He gives us victory over sin and death through our Lord Jesus Christ.

1 CORINTHIANS 15:55-57, NLT

Blessed be the God and Father of our Lord Jesus Christ, the Father of mercies and God of all comfort, who comforts us in all our affliction so that we will be able to comfort those who are in any affliction with the comfort with which we ourselves are comforted by God.

2 CORINTHIANS 1:3, 4, NASB

Yes, we are fully confident, and we would rather be away from these earthly bodies, for then we will be at home with the Lord.

2 CORINTHIANS 5:8, NLT

And now, dear brothers and sisters, we want you to know what will happen to the believers who have died so you will not grieve like people who have no hope. For since we believe that Jesus died and was raised to life again, we also believe that when Jesus returns, God will bring back with him the believers who have died.

1 THESSALONIANS 4:13, 14, NLT

Now may our Lord Jesus Christ himself and God our Father, who loved us and by his grace gave us eternal comfort and a wonderful hope, comfort you and strengthen you in every good thing you do and say.

2 THESSALONIANS 2:16, 17, NLT

For we do not have a High Priest who cannot sympathize with our weaknesses, but was in all points tempted as we are, yet without sin. Let us therefore come boldly to the throne of grace, that we may obtain mercy and find grace to help in time of need.

HEBREWS 4:15, 16, NKJV

Cast all your anxiety on him because he cares for you.

1 PETER 5:7, NIV

And God will wipe away every tear from their eyes; there shall be no more death, nor sorrow, nor crying. There shall be no more pain, for the former things have passed away.

REVELATION 21:4, NKJV

Overcoming Difficulty

And we know that all things work together for good to those who love God, to those who are the called according to His purpose.

ROMANS 8:28, NKJV

I'm absolutely convinced that nothing—nothing living or dead, angelic or demonic, today or tomorrow, high or low, thinkable or unthinkable—absolutely *nothing* can get between us and God's love because of the way that Jesus our Master has embraced us.

ROMANS 8:38, 39, MSG

For this reason I suffer as I do. However, I'm not ashamed. I know whom I trust. I'm convinced that he is able to protect what he had entrusted to me until that day. With faith and love for Christ Jesus, consider what you heard me say to be the pattern of accurate teachings.

2 TIMOTHY 1:12, 13, GOD'S WORD

When men are brought low and you say, "Lift them up!" then he will save the downcast.

JOB 22:29, NIV

It is better to trust in the Lord than to put confidence in man.

PSALM 118:8, KJV

With all these things in mind, dear brothers and sisters, stand firm and keep a strong grip on the teaching we passed on to you both in person and by letter. Now may our Lord Jesus Christ himself and God our Father, who loved us and by his grace gave us eternal comfort and a wonderful hope, comfort you and strengthen you in every good thing you do and say.

2 THESSALONIANS 2:15-17, NLT

But the Lord is faithful, who will establish you and guard you from the evil one. And we have confidence in the Lord concerning you, both that you do and will do the things we command you. Now may the Lord direct your hearts into the love of God and into the patience of Christ.

2 THESSALONIANS 3:3-5, NKJV

He was despised and rejected—a man of sorrows, acquainted with deepest grief. We turned our backs on him and looked the other way. He was despised, and we did not care. Yet it was our weaknesses he carried; it was our sorrows that weighed him down. And we thought his troubles were a punishment from God, a punishment for his own sins! But he was pierced for our rebellion, crushed for our sins. He was beaten so we could be whole. He was whipped so we could be healed. All of us, like sheep, have strayed away. We have left God's paths to follow our own. Yet the Lord laid on him the sins of us all.

ISAIAH 53:3-6, NLT

"Don't be afraid, because I am with you. Don't be intimidated; I am your God. I will strengthen you. I will help you. I will support you with my victorious right hand."

ISAIAH 41:10, GOD'S WORD

Loudly, I cry to the Lord. Loudly, I plead with the Lord for mercy. I pour out my complaints in his presence and tell him my troubles. When I begin to lose hope, you already know what I am experiencing. My enemies have hidden a trap for me on the path where I walk. Look to my right and see that no one notices me. Escape is impossible for me. No one cares about me. I call out to you, O Lord. I say, "You are my refuge, my own inheritance in this world of the living." Pay attention to my cry for help because I am very weak. Rescue me from those who pursue me because they are too strong for me. Release my soul from prison so that I may give thanks to your name. Righteous people will surround me because you are good to me.

PSALM 142:1-7, GOD'S WORD

Tell those rich in this world's wealth to quit being so full of themselves and so obsessed with money, which is here today and gone tomorrow. Tell them to go after God, who piles on all the riches we could ever manage— to do good, to be rich in helping others, to be extravagantly generous. If they do that, they'll build a treasury that will last, gaining life that is truly life.

1 TIMOTHY 6:17-19, MSG

When I was desperate, I called out, and God got me out of a tight spot. God's angel sets up a circle of protection around us while we pray. Open your mouth and taste, open your eyes and see—how good God is. Blessed are you who run to him. Worship God if you want the best; worship opens doors to all his goodness. Young lions on the prowl get hungry, but God-seekers are full of God.

PSALM 34:6-10, MSG

"And if God cares so wonderfully for flowers that are here today and thrown into the fire tomorrow, he will certainly care for you. Why do you have so little faith? And don't be concerned about what to eat and what to drink. Don't worry about such things. These things dominate the thoughts of unbelievers all over the world, but your Father already knows your needs. Seek the Kingdom of God above all else, and he will give you everything you need."

LUKE 12:28-31, NLT

When angry, do not sin; do not ever let your wrath (your exasperation, your fury or indignation) last until the sun goes down. Leave no [such] room or foothold for the devil [give no opportunity to him].

EPHESIANS 4:26, 27, AMP

"To him who overcomes I will grant to sit with Me on My throne, as I also overcame and sat down with My Father on His throne."

REVELATION 3:21, NKJV

Keep a cool head. Stay alert. The Devil is poised to pounce, and would like nothing better than to catch you napping. Keep your guard up. You're not the only ones plunged into these hard times. It's the same with Christians all over the world. So keep a firm grip on the faith. The suffering won't last forever. It won't be long before this generous God who has great plans for us in Christ—eternal and glorious plans they are!—will have you put together and on your feet for good.

1 PETER 5:8-10, MSG

"When the foundations of life are undermined, what can a righteous person do?" The Lord is in his holy temple. The Lord's throne is in heaven. His eyes see. They examine Adam's descendants. The Lord tests righteous people, but he hates wicked people and the ones who love violence. He rains down fire and burning sulfur upon wicked people. He makes them drink from a cup filled with scorching wind. The Lord is righteous. He loves a righteous way of life. Decent people will see his face.

PSALM 11:3-7 GOD'S WORD

But we have this treasure in jars of clay to show that this all-surpassing power is from God and not from us. We are hard pressed on every side, but not crushed; perplexed, but not in despair; persecuted, but not abandoned; struck down, but not destroyed.

2 CORINTHIANS 4:7-9, NIV

That is why we never give up. Though our bodies are dying, our spirits are being renewed every day. For our present troubles are small and won't last very long. Yet they produce for us a glory that vastly outweighs them and will last forever! So we don't look at the troubles we can see now; rather, we fix our gaze on things that cannot be seen. For the things we see now will soon be gone, but the things we cannot see will last forever.

2 CORINTHIANS 4:16-18, NLT

[The Lord God says] And the redeemed of the Lord shall return and come with singing to Zion; everlasting joy shall be upon their heads. They shall obtain joy and gladness, and sorrow and sighing shall flee away.

ISAIAH 51:11, AMP

Don't fret or worry. Instead of worrying, pray. Let petitions and praises shape your worries into prayers, letting God know your concerns. Before you know it, a sense of God's wholeness, everything coming together for good, will come and settle you down. It's wonderful what happens when Christ displaces worry at the center of your life.

Summing it all up, friends, I'd say you'll do best by filling your minds and meditating on things true, noble,
reputable, authentic, compelling, gracious—the best,
not the worst; the beautiful, not the ugly; things to
praise, not things to curse.

PHILIPPIANS 4:6-8 MSG

Even though I walk into the middle of trouble, you
guard my life against the anger of my enemies. You
stretch out your hand, and your right hand saves me.

PSALM 138:7, GOD'S WORD

"Let not your heart be troubled; you believe in God,
believe also in Me."

JOHN 14:1, NKJV

"Peace I leave with you; My peace I give to you; not as
the world gives do I give to you. Do not let your heart
be troubled, nor let it be fearful."

JOHN 14:27, NASB

So do not throw away your confidence; it will be rich-
ly rewarded. You need to persevere so that when you
have done the will of God, you will receive what he
has promised.

HEBREWS 10:35, 36, NIV

And I am convinced and sure of this very thing, that
He Who began a good work in you will continue until
the day of Jesus Christ [right up to the time of His
return], developing [that good work] and perfecting
and bringing it to full completion in you.

PHILIPPIANS 1:6, AMP

So let's not get tired of doing what is good. At just the right time we will reap a harvest of blessing if we don't give up.

GALATIANS 6:9, NLT

Be strong and let your heart take courage, all you who hope in the Lord.

PSALM 31:24, NASB

Sickness

And He said, "If you will give earnest heed to the voice of the Lord your God, and do what is right in His sight, and give ear to His commandments, and keep all His statutes, I will put none of the diseases on you which I have put on the Egyptians; for I, the Lord, am your healer."

EXODUS 15:26, NASB

Who forgives all your iniquities, who heals all your diseases.

PSALM 103:3, NKJV

He sent his word, and healed them, and delivered them from their destructions.

PSALM 107:20, KJV

But he was pierced for our transgressions, he was crushed for our iniquities; the punishment that brought us peace was upon him, and by his wounds we are healed.

ISAIAH 53:5, NIV

Heal me, O Lord, and I shall be healed; save me and I shall be saved, for You are my praise.

JEREMIAH 17:14, AMP

"For I will restore you to health and I will heal you of your wounds," declares the Lord.

JEREMIAH 30:17, NASB

Dear friend, listen well to my words; tune your ears to my voice. Keep my message in plain view at all times. Concentrate! Learn it by heart! Those who discover these words live, really live; body and soul, they're bursting with health.

PROVERBS 4:20-22, MSG

But the centurion said, "Lord, I am not worthy for You to come under my roof, but just say the word, and my servant will be healed."

MATTHEW 8:8, NASB

Jesus was going through all the cities and villages, teaching in their synagogues and proclaiming the gospel of the kingdom, and healing every kind of disease and every kind of sickness.

MATTHEW 9:35, NASB

And all the people were trying to touch Him, for power was coming from Him and healing them all.

LUKE 6:19, NASB

Jesus Christ is the same yesterday and today and forever.

HEBREWS 13:8, NASB

Is anyone among you sick? Let him call for the elders of the church, and let them pray over him, anointing him with oil in the name of the Lord. And the prayer of faith will save the sick, and the Lord will raise him up. And if he has committed sins, he will be forgiven.

JAMES 5:14, 15, NKJV

Who Himself bore our sins in His own body on the tree, that we, having died to sins, might live for righteousness—by whose stripes you were healed.

1 PETER 2:24, NKJV

Beloved, I pray that you may prosper in all things and be in health, just as your soul prospers.

3 JOHN 2, NKJV

Suffering

Enjoy prosperity while you can, but when hard times strike, realize that both come from God. Remember that nothing is certain in this life.

ECCLESIASTES 7:14, NLT

We can rejoice, too, when we run into problems and trials, for we know that they help us develop endurance.

ROMANS 5:3, NLT

And if children, then heirs; heirs of God, and joint-heirs with Christ; if so be that we suffer with him, that we may be also glorified together.

ROMANS 8:17, KJV

For you have been given not only the privilege of trusting in Christ but also the privilege of suffering for him.

PHILIPPIANS 1:29, NLT

So never be ashamed to tell others about our Lord. And don't be ashamed of me, either, even though I'm in prison for him. With the strength God gives you, be ready to suffer with me for the sake of the Good News.

2 TIMOTHY 1:8, NLT

For to this you were called, because Christ also suffered for us, leaving us an example, that you should follow His steps.

1 PETER 2:21, NKJV

But even if you suffer for doing what God approves, you are blessed. Don't be afraid of those who want to harm you. Don't get upset. But dedicate your lives to Christ as Lord. Always be ready to defend your confidence in God when anyone asks you to explain it. However, make your defense with gentleness and respect. Keep your conscience clear. Then those who treat the good Christian life you live with contempt will feel ashamed that they have ridiculed you. After all, if it is God's will, it's better to suffer for doing good than for doing wrong.

1 PETER 3:14-17, GOD'S WORD

However, if you suffer as a Christian, do not be ashamed, but praise God that you bear that name.

1 PETER 4:16, NIV

But may the God of all grace, who called us to His eternal glory by Christ Jesus, after you have suffered a while, perfect, establish, strengthen, and settle you.

1 PETER 5:10, NKJV

For in the day of trouble He will hide me in His shelter; in the secret place of His tent will He hide me; He will set me high upon a rock.

PSALM 27:5, AMP

I want to know Christ and experience the mighty power that raised him from the dead. I want to suffer with him, sharing in his death.

PHILIPPIANS 3:10, NLT

God is our refuge and strength, a very present help in trouble.

PSALM 46:1, KJV

Temptation

Your word have I treasured in my heart, that I may not sin against You.

PSALM 119:11, NASB

He who covers his sins will not prosper, but whoever confesses and forsakes them will have mercy.

PROVERBS 28:13, NKJV

For sin shall not have dominion over you, for you are not under law but under grace.

ROMANS 6:14, NKJV

So, people who think they are standing firmly should be careful that they don't fall. There isn't any temptation that you have experienced which is unusual for humans. God, who faithfully keeps his promises, will not allow you to be tempted beyond your power to resist. But when you are tempted, he will also give you the ability to endure the temptation as your way of escape.

1 CORINTHIANS 10:12, 13, GOD'S WORD

Finally, be strong in the Lord and in the strength of His might. Put on the full armor of God, so that you will be able to stand firm against the schemes of the devil. In addition to all, taking up the shield of faith with which you will be able to extinguish all the flaming arrows of the evil one.

EPHESIANS 6:10, 11, 16, NASB

For since He Himself was tempted in that which He has suffered, He is able to come to the aid of those who are tempted.

HEBREWS 2:18, NASB

Seeing then that we have a great High Priest who has passed through the heavens, Jesus the Son of God, let us hold fast our confession. For we do not have a High Priest who cannot sympathize with our weaknesses, but was in all points tempted as we are, yet without sin. Let us therefore come boldly to the throne of grace, that we may obtain mercy and find grace to help in time of need.

HEBREWS 4:14-16, NKJV

Dear brothers and sisters, when troubles come your way, consider it an opportunity for great joy. For you know that when your faith is tested, your endurance has a chance to grow. God blesses those who patiently endure testing and temptation. Afterward they will receive the crown of life that God has promised to those who love him.

JAMES 1:2, 3, 12, NLT

Let no one say when he is tempted, "I am tempted by God"; for God cannot be tempted by evil, nor does He Himself tempt anyone. But each one is tempted when he is drawn away by his own desires and enticed.

JAMES 1:13, 14, NKJV

Submit yourselves therefore to God. Resist the devil, and he will flee from you.

JAMES 4:7, KJV

You are extremely happy about these things, even though you have to suffer different kinds of trouble for a little while now. The purpose of these troubles is to test your faith as fire tests how genuine gold is. Your faith is more precious than gold, and by passing the test, it gives praise, glory, and honor to God. This will happen when Jesus Christ appears again.

1 PETER 1:6, 7, GOD'S WORD

Keep a cool head. Stay alert. The Devil is poised to pounce, and would like nothing better than to catch you napping. Keep your guard up. You're not the only ones plunged into these hard times. It's the same with Christians all over the world. So keep a firm grip on the faith.

1 PETER 5:8, 9, MSG

Then the Lord knows how to rescue the godly from temptation.

2 PETER 2:9, NASB

If we confess our sins, he is faithful and just to forgive us our sins, and to cleanse us from all unrighteousness.

1 JOHN 1:9, KJV

You are of God, little children, and have overcome them, because He who is in you is greater than he who is in the world.

1 JOHN 4:4, NKJV

And now to him who can keep you on your feet, standing tall in his bright presence, fresh and celebrating—to our one God, our only Savior, through Jesus Christ, our Master, be glory, majesty, strength, and rule before all time, and now, and to the end of all time. Yes.

JUDE 24, 25, MSG

Section 3

The Living Word for Living Life When You Need Wisdom in Practical Matters

Business

Money

Success

Wisdom

Business

"This book of the law shall not depart from your mouth, but you shall meditate on it day and night, so that you may be careful to do according to all that is written in it; for then you will make your way prosperous, and then you will have success."

JOSHUA 1:8, NASB

Thus says the Lord, your Redeemer, the Holy One of Israel, "I am the Lord your God, who teaches you to profit, who leads you in the way you should go."

ISAIAH 48:17, NASB

Beloved, I pray that you may prosper in all things and be in health, just as your soul prospers.

3 JOHN 2, NKJV

But remember the Lord your God, for it is he who gives you the ability to produce wealth, and so confirms his covenant, which he swore to your forefathers, as it is today.

DEUTERONOMY 8:18, NIV

Trust in the Lord with all your heart; do not depend on your own understanding. Seek his will in all you do, and he will show you which path to take. Don't be impressed with your own wisdom. Instead, fear the Lord and turn away from evil. Then you will have healing for your body and strength for your bones. Honor the Lord with your wealth and with the best part of everything you produce. Then he will fill your barns with grain, and your vats will overflow with good wine.

PROVERBS 3:5-10, NLT

"For you will be successful if you carefully obey the decrees and regulations that the Lord gave to Israel through Moses. Be strong and courageous; do not be afraid or lose heart!"

1 CHRONICLES 22:13, NLT

Blessed is the man who does not walk in the counsel of the wicked or stand in the way of sinners or sit in the seat of mockers. But his delight is in the law of the Lord, and on his law he meditates day and night. He is like a tree planted by streams of water, which yields its fruit in season and whose leaf does not wither. Whatever he does prospers.

PSALM 1:1-3, NIV

But seek first the kingdom of God and His righteousness, and all these things shall be added to you.

MATTHEW 6:33, NKJV

Put God in charge of your work, then what you've planned will take place.

PROVERBS 16:3, MSG

Through skillful and godly Wisdom is a house (a life, a home, a family) built, and by understanding it is established [on a sound and good foundation], and by knowledge shall its chambers [of every area] be filled with all precious and pleasant riches.

PROVERBS 24:3, 4, AMP

And keep the charge of the Lord your God: to walk in His ways, to keep His statutes, His commandments, His judgments, and His testimonies, as it is written in the Law of Moses, that you may prosper in all that you do and wherever you turn.

1 KINGS 2:3, NKJV

If they obey and serve Him, they shall spend their days in prosperity, and their years in pleasures.

JOB 36:11, NKJV

Masters, treat your servants considerably. Be fair with them. Don't forget for a minute that you, too, serve a Master—God in heaven.

COLOSSIANS 4:1, MSG

But we urge you, brethren, to excel still more, and to make it your ambition to lead a quiet life and attend to your own business and work with your hands, just as we commanded you, so that you will behave properly toward outsiders and not be in any need.

1 THESSALONIANS 4:10-12, NASB

Money

Don't wear yourself out trying to get rich. Be wise enough to know when to quit.

In the blink of an eye wealth disappears, for it will sprout wings and fly away like an eagle.

PROVERBS 23:4, 5, NLT

It is better to be godly and have little than to be evil and rich.

PSALM 37:16, NLT

Listen, my dear brothers and sisters! Didn't God choose poor people in the world to become rich in faith and to receive the kingdom that he promised to those who love him?

JAMES 2:5, GOD'S WORD

One hand full of rest is better than two fists full of labor and striving after wind.

ECCLESIASTES 4:6, NASB

"Because of the devastation of the afflicted, because of the groaning of the needy, now I will arise," says the Lord; "I will set him in the safety for which he longs."

PSALM 12:5, NASB

Whoever makes fun of a poor person insults his maker. Whoever is happy to see someone's distress will not escape punishment.

PROVERBS 17:5, GOD'S WORD

Don't rob the poor just because you can, or exploit the needy in court.

PROVERBS 22:22, NLT

Tell those rich in this world's wealth to quit being so full of themselves and so obsessed with money, which is here today and gone tomorrow. Tell them to go after God, who piles on all the riches we could ever manage—to do good, to be rich in helping others, to be extravagantly generous. If they do that, they'll build a treasury that will last, gaining life that is truly life.

1 TIMOTHY 6:17-19, MSG

People who work hard sleep well, whether they eat little or much. But the rich seldom get a good night's sleep. There is another serious problem I have seen under the sun. Hoarding riches harms the saver. Money is put into risky investments that turn sour, and everything is lost. In the end, there is nothing left to pass on to one's children.

ECCLESIASTES 5:12-14, NLT

But remember the Lord your God, for it is he who gives you the ability to produce wealth, and so confirms his covenant, which he swore to your forefathers, as it is today.

DEUTERONOMY 8:18, NIV

Needy people will not always be forgotten. Nor will the hope of oppressed people be lost forever.

PSALM 9:18, GOD'S WORD

"But he saves other people from their slander and the needy from the power of the mighty. Then the poor have hope while wrongdoing shuts its mouth."

JOB 5:15, 16, GOD'S WORD

He who leans on, trusts in, and is confident in his riches shall fall, but the [uncompromisingly] righteous shall flourish like a green bough.

PROVERBS 11:28, AMP

A faithful man shall abound with blessings, but he who makes haste to be rich [at any cost] shall not go unpunished.

PROVERBS 28:20, AMP

Riches won't help on the day of judgment, but right living can save you from death.

PROVERBS 11:4, NLT

One person pretends to be rich but has nothing. Another pretends to be poor but has great wealth.

PROVERBS 13:7, GOD'S WORD

He who loves money will not be satisfied with money, nor he who loves abundance with its income. This too is vanity.

ECCLESIASTES 5:10, NASB

A person who gets ahead by oppressing the poor or by showering gifts on the rich will end in poverty.

PROVERBS 22:16, NLT

Greedy people try to get rich quick but don't realize they're headed for poverty.

PROVERBS 28:22, NLT

The rich and the poor have this in common, the Lord is the maker of them all.

PROVERBS 22:2, NKJV

But those who suffer he delivers in their suffering; he speaks to them in their affliction.

JOB 36:15, NIV

Better is a little with the fear of the Lord, than great treasure with trouble.

PROVERBS 15:16, NKJV

Better is the poor who walks in his integrity than he who is crooked though he be rich.

PROVERBS 28:6, NASB

How blessed is he who considers the helpless; the Lord will deliver him in a day of trouble.

PSALM 41:1, NASB

Success

Great wealth is in the house of the righteous, but trouble is in the income of the wicked.

PROVERBS 15:6, NASB

True humility and fear of the Lord lead to riches, honor, and long life.

PROVERBS 22:4, NLT

"Then the Lord your God will prosper you abundantly in all the work of your hand, in the offspring of your body and in the offspring of your cattle and in the produce of your ground, for the Lord will again rejoice over you for good, just as He rejoiced over your fathers."

DEUTERONOMY 30:9, NASB

Then He will give the rain for your seed with which you sow the ground, and bread of the increase of the earth; it will be fat and plentiful. In that day your cattle will feed in large pastures.

ISAIAH 30:23, NKJV

Moreover, that every man who eats and drinks sees good in all his labor—it is the gift of God.

ECCLESIASTES 3:13, NASB

"The Lord will make you abound in prosperity, in the offspring of your body and in the offspring of your beast and in the produce of your ground, in the land which the Lord swore to your fathers to give you. The Lord will open for you His good storehouse, the heavens, to give rain to your land in its season and to bless all the work of your hand; and you shall lend to many nations, but you shall not borrow. The Lord will make you the head and not the tail, and you only will be above, and you will not be underneath, if you listen to the commandments of the Lord your God, which I charge you today, to observe them carefully."

DEUTERONOMY 28:11-13, NASB

It is a gift from God when God gives some people wealth and possessions, the power to enjoy them, the ability to accept their lot in life, and the ability to rejoice in their own hard work.

ECCLESIASTES 5:19, GOD'S WORD

Riches and honor are with me, enduring riches and righteousness. My fruit is better than gold, yes, than fine gold, and my revenue than choice silver.

PROVERBS 8:18, 19, NKJV

Wealth and riches are in his house, and his righteousness endures forever.

PSALM 112:3, NIV

"If you give up your lust for money and throw your precious gold into the river, the Almighty himself will be your treasure. He will be your precious silver!"

JOB 22:24, 25, NLT

They will build houses and live there. They will plant vineyards and eat fruit from them. They will not build homes and have others live there. They will not plant and have others eat from it. My people will live as long as trees, and my chosen ones will enjoy what they've done. They will never again work for nothing. They will never again give birth to children who die young, because they will be offspring blessed by the Lord.

ISAIAH 65:21-23, GOD'S WORD

"All these blessings will come upon you and overtake you if you obey the Lord your God: Blessed shall you be in the city, and blessed shall you be in the country. Blessed shall be the offspring of your body and the produce of your ground and the offspring of your beasts, the increase of your herd and the young of your flock. Blessed shall be your basket and your kneading bowl. Blessed shall you be when you come in, and blessed shall you be when you go out."

DEUTERONOMY 28:2-6, NASB

Wisdom

If you need wisdom, ask our generous God, and he will give it to you. He will not rebuke you for asking.

JAMES 1:5, NLT

Many people shall come and say, "Come, and let us go up to the mountain of the Lord, to the house of the God of Jacob; He will teach us His ways, and we shall walk in His paths." For out of Zion shall go forth the law, and the word of the Lord from Jerusalem.

ISAIAH 2:3, NKJV

For God gives wisdom and knowledge and joy to a man who is good in His sight; but to the sinner He gives the work of gathering and collecting, that he may give to him who is good before God. This also is vanity and grasping for the wind.

ECCLESIASTES 2:26, NKJV

I will praise the Lord, who counsels me; even at night my heart instructs me.

PSALM 16:7, NIV

Then you will understand what it means to fear the Lord, and you will gain knowledge of God. For the Lord grants wisdom! From his mouth come knowledge and understanding.

PROVERBS 2:5, 6, NLT

Behold, You desire truth in the inner being; make me therefore to know wisdom in my inmost heart.

PSALM 51:6, AMP

And we know that the Son of God has come and has given us an understanding, that we may know Him who is true; and we are in Him who is true, in His Son Jesus Christ. This is the true God and eternal life.

1 JOHN 5:20, NKJV

For God, who said, "Let there be light in the darkness," has made this light shine in our hearts so we could know the glory of God that is seen in the face of Jesus Christ.

2 CORINTHIANS 4:6, NLT

Evil men do not understand justice, but those who seek the Lord understand all things.

PROVERBS 28:5, NASB

Section 4

The Living Word for Living Life While You're Waiting for Your Breakthrough

Contentment

God's Provision

Peace

Purpose

Strength

Waiting on God

Contentment

A cheerful heart is good medicine, but a crushed spirit dries up the bones.

PROVERBS 17:22, NIV

Every day is a terrible day for a miserable person, but a cheerful heart has a continual feast.

PROVERBS 15:15, GOD'S WORD

A devout life does bring wealth, but it's the rich simplicity of being yourself before God.

1 TIMOTHY 6:6, MSG

If they obey and serve Him, they shall spend their days in prosperity, and their years in pleasures.

JOB 36:11, NKJV

Rest in the Lord, and wait patiently for Him; do not fret because of him who prospers in his way, because of the man who brings wicked schemes to pass. Cease from anger, and forsake wrath; do not fret—it only causes harm.

PSALM 37:7, 8, NKJV

Satisfy us in the morning with your unfailing love, that we may sing for joy and be glad all our days.

PSALM 90:14, NIV

For He has satisfied the thirsty soul, and the hungry soul He has filled with what is good.

PSALM 107:9, NASB

The fear of the Lord leads to life, so that one may sleep satisfied, untouched by evil.

PROVERBS 19:23, NASB

Do not fret because of evildoers, nor be envious of the wicked;

PROVERBS 24:19, NKJV

"Why spend money on what is not bread, and your labor on what does not satisfy? Listen, listen to me, and eat what is good, and your soul will delight in the richest of fare."

ISAIAH 55:2, NIV

Not that I was ever in need, for I have learned how to be content with whatever I have. I know how to live on almost nothing or with everything. I have learned the secret of living in every situation, whether it is with a full stomach or empty, with plenty or little.

PHILIPPIANS 4:11, 12, NLT

But if we have food and clothing, with these we shall be content (satisfied).

1 TIMOTHY 6:8, AMP

Make sure that your character is free from the love of money, being content with what you have; for He Himself has said, "I will never desert you, nor will I ever forsake you."

HEBREWS 13:5, NASB

Because I am righteous, I will see you. When I awake, I will see you face to face and be satisfied.

PSALM 17:15, NLT

The poor will eat and be satisfied; they who seek the Lord will praise him—may your hearts live forever!

PSALM 22:26, NIV

With long life I will satisfy him and show him my salvation.

PSALM 91:16, NIV

Who satisfies your mouth [your necessity and desire at your personal age and situation] with good so that your youth, renewed, is like the eagle's [strong, overcoming, soaring]!

PSALM 103:5, AMP

Lazy people want much but get little, but those who work hard will prosper.

PROVERBS 13:4, NLT

He will not accept any compensation; he will refuse the bribe, however great it is.

PROVERBS 6:35, NIV

Then some soldiers asked him, "And what should we do?" He replied, "Don't extort money and don't accuse people falsely—be content with your pay."

LUKE 3:14, NIV

That is why, for Christ's sake, I delight in weaknesses, in insults, in hardships, in persecutions, in difficulties. For when I am weak, then I am strong.

2 CORINTHIANS 12:10, NIV

_____

God's Provision

And my God will supply all your needs according to His riches in glory in Christ Jesus.

PHILIPPIANS 4:19, NASB

I can do all things through Christ who strengthens me.

PHILIPPIANS 4:13, NKJV

Yet in all these things we are more than conquerors through Him who loved us.

ROMANS 8:37, NKJV

Therefore let no one boast in men. For all things are yours: whether Paul or Apollos or Cephas, or the world or life or death, or things present or things to come—all are yours. And you are Christ's, and Christ is God's.

1 CORINTHIANS 3:21-23, NKJV

"If you abide in Me, and My words abide in you, ask whatever you wish, and it will be done for you."

JOHN 15:7, NASB

"And in that day you will ask Me nothing. Most assuredly, I say to you, whatever you ask the Father in My name He will give you. Until now you have asked nothing in My name. Ask, and you will receive, that your joy may be full."

JOHN 16:23, 24, NKJV

"And all things you ask in prayer, believing, you will receive."

MATTHEW 21:22, NASB

"Therefore I tell you, whatever you ask for in prayer, believe that you have received it, and it will be yours."

MARK 11:24, NIV

Blessed be the God and Father of our Lord Jesus Christ, who has blessed us with every spiritual blessing in the heavenly places in Christ.

EPHESIANS 1:3, NASB

And we receive from Him whatever we ask, because we [watchfully] obey His orders [observe His suggestions and injunctions, follow His plan for us] and [habitually] practice what is pleasing to Him.

1 JOHN 3:22, AMP

For He made Him who knew no sin to be sin for us, that we might become the righteousness of God in Him.

2 CORINTHIANS 5:21, NKJV

For to me to live is Christ, and to die is gain.

PHILIPPIANS 1:21, KJV

This means that anyone who belongs to Christ has become a new person. The old life is gone; a new life has begun!

2 CORINTHIANS 5:17, NLT

Now to Him who is able to do far more abundantly beyond all that we ask or think, according to the power that works within us, to Him be the glory in the church and in Christ Jesus to all generations forever and ever. Amen.

EPHESIANS 3:20, 21, NASB

And God will generously provide all you need. Then you will always have everything you need and plenty left over to share with others.

2 CORINTHIANS 9:8, NLT

Blessed be the Lord, Who bears our burdens and carries us day by day, even the God Who is our salvation!

PSALM 68:19, AMP

Peace

I fall asleep in peace the moment I lie down because you alone, O Lord, enable me to live securely.

PSALM 4:8, GOD'S WORD

The Lord will give strength unto his people; the Lord will bless his people with peace.

PSALM 29:11, KJV

For to us a child is born, to us a son is given, and the government will be on his shoulders. And he will be called Wonderful Counselor, Mighty God, Everlasting Father, Prince of Peace. Of the increase of his government and peace there will be no end. He will reign on David's throne and over his kingdom, establishing and upholding it with justice and righteousness from that time on and forever. The zeal of the Lord Almighty will accomplish this.

ISAIAH 9:6, 7, NIV

You will keep in perfect peace all who trust in you, all whose thoughts are fixed on you!

ISAIAH 26:3, NLT

Lord, you establish peace for us; all that we have accomplished you have done for us.

ISAIAH 26:12, NIV

"Peace I leave with you; My peace I give to you; not as the world gives do I give to you. Do not let your heart be troubled, nor let it be fearful."

JOHN 14:27, NASB

Therefore being justified by faith, we have peace with God through our Lord Jesus Christ.

ROMANS 5:1, KJV

The God of peace will soon crush Satan under your feet. The grace of our Lord Jesus be with you.

ROMANS 16:20, NASB

But now you have been united with Christ Jesus. Once you were far away from God, but now you have been brought near to him through the blood of Christ. For Christ himself has brought peace to us. He united Jews and Gentiles into one people when, in his own body on the cross, he broke down the wall of hostility that separated us.

EPHESIANS 2:13, 14, NLT

Be anxious for nothing, but in everything by prayer and supplication with thanksgiving let your requests be made known to God. And the peace of God, which surpasses all comprehension, will guard your hearts and your minds in Christ Jesus. The things you have learned and received and heard and seen in me, practice these things, and the God of peace will be with you.

PHILIPPIANS 4:6, 7, 9, NASB

Let the peace of Christ rule in your hearts, to which indeed you were called in one body; and be thankful.

COLOSSIANS 3:15, NASB

Purpose

Let your eyes look directly ahead and let your gaze be fixed straight in front of you. Watch the path of your feet and all your ways will be established. Do not turn to the right nor to the left; turn your foot from evil.

PROVERBS 4:25-27, NASB

When people do not accept divine guidance, they run wild. But whoever obeys the law is joyful.

PROVERBS 29:18, NLT

Therefore I, a prisoner for serving the Lord, beg you to lead a life worthy of your calling, for you have been called by God. Always be humble and gentle. Be patient with each other, making allowance for each other's faults because of your love. Make every effort to keep yourselves united in the Spirit, binding yourselves together with peace.

EPHESIANS 4:1-3, NLT

I do not consider, brethren, that I have captured and made it my own [yet]; but one thing I do [it is my one aspiration]: forgetting what lies behind and straining forward to what lies ahead, I press on toward the goal to win the [supreme and heavenly] prize to which God in Christ Jesus is calling us upward.

PHILIPPIANS 3:13, 14, AMP

The naïve believes everything, but the sensible man considers his steps.

PROVERBS 14:15, NASB

Plans succeed through good counsel; don't go to war without wise advice.

PROVERBS 20:18, NLT

"Only be strong and very courageous; be careful to do according to all the law which Moses My servant commanded you; do not turn from it to the right or to the left, so that you may have success wherever you go."

JOSHUA 1:7, NASB

"You did not choose Me but I chose you, and appointed you that you would go and bear fruit, and that your fruit would remain, so that whatever you ask of the Father in My name He may give to you."

JOHN 15:16, NASB

Jesus came and told his disciples, "I have been given all authority in heaven and on earth. Therefore, go and make disciples of all the nations, baptizing them in the name of the Father and the Son and the Holy Spirit. Teach these new disciples to obey all the commands I have given you. And be sure of this: I am with you always, even to the end of the age."

MATTHEW 28:18-20, NLT

A man's mind plans his way, but the Lord directs his steps and makes them sure.

PROVERBS 16:9, AMP

I know, O Lord, that a man's life is not his own; it is not for man to direct his steps.

JEREMIAH 10:23, NIV

Trust in the Lord with all your heart; do not depend on your own understanding. Seek his will in all you do, and he will show you which path to take.

PROVERBS 3:5, 6, NLT

"But you will receive power when the Holy Spirit comes upon you. And you will be my witnesses, telling people about me everywhere—in Jerusalem, throughout Judea, in Samaria, and to the ends of the earth."

ACTS 1:8, NLT

To every thing there is a season, and a time to every purpose under the heaven.

ECCLESIASTES 3:1, KJV

"But rise and stand on your feet; for I have appeared to you for this purpose, to make you a minister and a witness both of the things which you have seen and of the things which I will yet reveal to you."

ACTS 26:16, NKJV

And we know that all things work together for good to those who love God, to those who are the called according to His purpose.

ROMANS 8:28, NKJV

Strength

Then [Ezra] told them, Go your way, eat the fat, drink the sweet drink, and send portions to him for whom nothing is prepared; for this day is holy to our Lord. And be not grieved and depressed, for the joy of the Lord is your strength and stronghold.

NEHEMIAH 8:10, AMP

The Lord is my rock and my fortress and my deliverer; my God, my strength, in whom I will trust;

PSALM 18:2, NKJV

The Lord is my Light and my Salvation—whom shall I fear or dread? The Lord is the Refuge and Stronghold of my life—of whom shall I be afraid?

PSALM 27:1, AMP

My soul weeps because of grief; strengthen me according to Your word.

PSALM 119:28, NASB

Counsel is mine, and sound wisdom: I am understanding; I have strength.

PROVERBS 8:14, KJV

For thus says the Lord God, the Holy One of Israel: "In returning and rest you shall be saved; in quietness and confidence shall be your strength."

ISAIAH 30:15, NKJV

He gives power to the faint and weary, and to him who has no might He increases strength [causing it to multiply and making it to abound].

ISAIAH 40:29, AMP

But those who hope in the Lord will renew their strength. They will soar on wings like eagles; they will run and not grow weary, they will walk and not be faint.

ISAIAH 40:31, NIV

"Don't be afraid, because I am with you. Don't be intimidated; I am your God. I will strengthen you. I will help you. I will support you with my victorious right hand."

ISAIAH 41:10, GOD'S WORD

And he said, "O man greatly beloved, fear not! Peace be to you; be strong, yes, be strong!" So when he spoke to me I was strengthened, and said, "Let my lord speak, for you have strengthened me."

DANIEL 10:19, NKJV

I'm asking God to give you a gift from the wealth of his glory. I pray that he would give you inner strength and power through his Spirit. Then Christ will live in you through faith. I also pray that love may be the ground into which you sink your roots and on which you have your foundation.

EPHESIANS 3:16, 17, GOD'S WORD

Finally, my brethren, be strong in the Lord, and in the power of his might.

EPHESIANS 6:10, KJV

Therefore put on the full armor of God, so that when the day of evil comes, you may be able to stand your ground, and after you have done everything, to stand.

EPHESIANS 6:13, NIV

I can do all things through Christ who strengthens me.

PHILIPPIANS 4:13, NKJV

And we pray this in order that you may live a life worthy of the Lord and may please him in every way: bearing fruit in every good work, growing in the knowledge of God, being strengthened with all power according to his glorious might so that you may have great endurance and patience, and joyfully giving thanks to the Father, who has qualified you to share in the inheritance of the saints in the kingdom of light.

COLOSSIANS 1:10-12, NIV

Waiting on God

Our soul waits for the Lord; He is our help and shield.

PSALM 33:20, NASB

"The vision will still happen at the appointed time. It hurries toward its goal. It won't be a lie. If it's delayed, wait for it. It will certainly happen. It won't be late."

HABAKKUK 2:3, GOD'S WORD

Let us hold unswervingly to the hope we profess, for he who promised is faithful.

HEBREWS 10:23, NIV

After all, we will remain Christ's partners only if we continue to hold on to our original confidence until the end.

HEBREWS 3:14, GOD'S WORD

In that day the people will proclaim, "This is our God! We trusted in him, and he saved us! This is the Lord, in whom we trusted. Let us rejoice in the salvation he brings!"

ISAIAH 25:9, NLT

Rest in the Lord, and wait patiently for Him; do not fret because of him who prospers in his way, because of the man who brings wicked schemes to pass. Cease from anger, and forsake wrath; do not fret—it only causes harm. For evildoers shall be cut off; but those who wait on the Lord, they shall inherit the earth.

PSALM 37:7-9, NKJV

I waited patiently for the Lord; he turned to me and heard my cry. He lifted me out of the slimy pit, out of the mud and mire; he set my feet on a rock and gave me a firm place to stand. He put a new song in my mouth, a hymn of praise to our God. Many will see and fear and put their trust in the Lord.

PSALM 40:1-3, NIV

Therefore the Lord longs to be gracious to you, and therefore He waits on high to have compassion on you. For the Lord is a God of justice; how blessed are all those who long for Him.

ISAIAH 30:18, NASB

No one who trusts in you will ever be disgraced, but disgrace comes to those who try to deceive others. Show me the right path, O Lord; point out the road for me to follow. Lead me by your truth and teach me, for you are the God who saves me. All day long I put my hope in you.

PSALM 25:3-5, NLT

Wait for the Lord; be strong and let your heart take courage; yes, wait for the Lord.

PSALM 27:14, NASB

The Lord is good to those who wait for Him, to the person who seeks Him. It is good that He waits silently for the salvation of the Lord.

LAMENTATIONS 3:25, 26, NASB

Therefore I will look unto the Lord; I will wait for the God of my salvation: my God will hear me.

MICAH 7:7, KJV

Wait calmly for God alone, my soul, because my hope comes from him. He alone is my rock and my savior— my stronghold. I cannot be shaken.

PSALM 62:5, 6, GOD'S WORD

The Lord supports everyone who falls. He straightens the backs of those who are bent over. The eyes of all creatures look to you, and you give them their food at the proper time.

PSALM 145:14, 15, GOD'S WORD

I pray to God—my life a prayer—and wait for what he'll say and do. My life's on the line before God, my Lord, waiting and watching till morning, waiting and watching till morning.

PSALM 130:5, 6, MSG

So you, by the help of your God, return; observe mercy and justice, and wait on your God continually.

HOSEA 12:6, NKJV

Section 5

The Living Word for Living Life When You're Struggling with Negative Emotions and Experiences

Anger

Envy

Stress

Worry

Anger

Cease from anger, and forsake wrath; do not fret—it only causes harm.

PSALM 37:8, NKJV

A wise person is cautious and turns away from evil, but a fool is careless and overconfident. A short-tempered person acts stupidly, and a person who plots evil is hated.

PROVERBS 14:16, 17, GOD'S WORD

People with understanding control their anger; a hot temper shows great foolishness.

PROVERBS 14:29, NLT

A gentle answer turns away wrath, but a harsh word stirs up anger.

PROVERBS 15:1, NASB

He who is slow to anger is better than the mighty, and he who rules his spirit than he who takes a city.

PROVERBS 16:32, NKJV

Don't be quick to get angry, because anger is typical of fools.

ECCLESIASTES 7:9, GOD'S WORD

"I'm telling you that anyone who is so much as angry with a brother or sister is guilty of murder. Carelessly call a brother 'idiot!' and you just might find yourself hauled into court. Thoughtlessly yell 'stupid!' at a sister and you are on the brink of hellfire. The simple moral fact is that words kill. This is how I want you to conduct yourself in these matters. If you enter your place of worship and, about to make an offering, you suddenly remember a grudge a friend has against you, abandon your offering, leave immediately, go to this friend and make things right. Then and only then, come back and work things out with God."

MATTHEW 5:22-24, MSG

"For if you forgive others for their transgressions, your heavenly Father will also forgive you."

MATTHEW 6:14, NASB

Do not take revenge, my friends, but leave room for God's wrath, for it is written: "It is mine to avenge; I will repay," says the Lord. On the contrary: "If your enemy is hungry, feed him; if he is thirsty, give him something to drink. In doing this, you will heap burning coals on his head." Do not be overcome by evil, but overcome evil with good.

ROMANS 12:19-21, NIV

When angry, do not sin; do not ever let your wrath (your exasperation, your fury or indignation) last until the sun goes down.

EPHESIANS 4:26, AMP

Make a clean break with all cutting, backbiting, profane talk. Be gentle with one another, sensitive. Forgive one another as quickly and thoroughly as God in Christ forgave you.

EPHESIANS 4:31, 32, MSG

But now you yourselves are to put off all these: anger, wrath, malice, blasphemy, filthy language out of your mouth.

COLOSSIANS 3:8, NKJV

For we know Him who said, "Vengeance is Mine, I will repay." And again, "The Lord will judge His people."

HEBREWS 10:30, NASB

This you know, my beloved brethren. But everyone must be quick to hear, slow to speak and slow to anger; for the anger of man does not achieve the righteousness of God.

JAMES 1:19, 20, NASB

———————

Envy

Surely resentment destroys the fool, and jealousy kills the simple.

JOB 5:2, NLT

Do not fret because of evil men or be envious of those who do wrong.

PSALM 37:1, NIV

A sound heart is the life of the flesh: but envy the rottenness of the bones.

PROVERBS 14:30, KJV

Do not let your heart envy sinners, but live in the fear of the Lord always.

PROVERBS 23:17, NASB

Don't envy evil people or desire their company.

PROVERBS 24:1, NLT

Then I observed all the work and ambition motivated by envy. What a waste! Smoke. And spitting into the wind.

ECCLESIASTES 4:4, MSG

And then he added, "It is what comes from inside that defiles you. For from within, out of a person's heart, come evil thoughts, sexual immorality, theft, murder, adultery, greed, wickedness, deceit, lustful desires, envy, slander, pride, and foolishness."

MARK 7:20-22, NLT

Love is patient, love is kind. It does not envy, it does not boast, it is not proud.

1 CORINTHIANS 13:4, NIV

When you follow the desires of your sinful nature, the results are very clear: sexual immorality, impurity, lustful pleasures, idolatry, sorcery, hostility, quarreling, jealousy, outbursts of anger, selfish ambition, dissension, division, envy, drunkenness, wild parties, and other sins like these. Let me tell you again, as I have before, that anyone living that sort of life will not inherit the Kingdom of God.

GALATIANS 5:19-21, NLT

For we ourselves were also once foolish, disobedient, deceived, serving various lusts and pleasures, living in malice and envy, hateful and hating one another.

TITUS 3:3, NKJV

But if you are bitterly jealous and there is selfish ambition in your heart, don't cover up the truth with boasting and lying. For jealousy and selfishness are not God's kind of wisdom. Such things are earthly, unspiritual, and demonic. For wherever there is jealousy and selfish ambition, there you will find disorder and evil of every kind.

JAMES 3:14-16, NLT

Therefore, rid yourselves of all malice and all deceit, hypocrisy, envy, and slander of every kind.

1 PETER 2:1, NIV

Do not envy a man of violence and do not choose any of his ways.

PROVERBS 3:31, NASB

Do not fret because of evildoers, nor be envious of the wicked.

PROVERBS 24:19, NKJV

If anyone teaches false doctrines and does not agree to the sound instruction of our Lord Jesus Christ and to godly teaching, he is conceited and understands nothing. He has an unhealthy interest in controversies and quarrels about words that result in envy, strife, malicious talk, evil suspicions.

1 TIMOTHY 6:3, 4, NIV

Stress

Cast all your anxiety on him because he cares for you.

1 PETER 5:7, NIV

No test or temptation that comes your way is beyond the course of what others have had to face. All you need to remember is that God will never let you down; he'll never let you be pushed past your limit; he'll always be there to help you come through it.

1 CORINTHIANS 10:13, MSG

Anxiety in a man's heart weighs it down, but a good word makes it glad.

PROVERBS 12:25, NASB

Let your light so shine before men, that they may see your good works, and glorify your Father which is in heaven.

MATTHEW 5:16, KJV

I look up to the mountains; does my strength come from mountains?

No, my strength comes from God, who made heaven, and earth, and mountains.

He won't let you stumble, your Guardian God won't fall asleep. Not on your life! Israel's Guardian will never doze or sleep. God's your Guardian, right at your side to protect you—shielding you from sunstroke, sheltering you from moonstroke. God guards you from every evil, he guards your very life. He guards you when you leave and when you return, he guards you now, he guards you always.

PSALM 121:1-8, MSG

In every thing give thanks: for this is the will of God in Christ Jesus concerning you.

1 THESSALONIANS 5:18, KJV

Be anxious for nothing, but in everything by prayer and supplication with thanksgiving let your requests be made known to God. And the peace of God, which surpasses all comprehension, will guard your hearts and your minds in Christ Jesus.

PHILIPPIANS 4:6, 7, NASB

"Peace I leave with you; My peace I give to you; not as

the world gives do I give to you. Do not let your heart be troubled, nor let it be fearful."

JOHN 14:27, NASB

God is our refuge and strength, a very present help in trouble. Therefore we will not fear,

even though the earth be removed, and though the mountains be carried into the midst of the sea; though its waters roar and be troubled, though the mountains shake with its swelling.

PSALM 46:1-3, NKJV

The Lord also will be a refuge for the oppressed, a refuge in times of trouble. And those who know Your name will put their trust in You; for You, Lord, have not forsaken those who seek You.

PSALM 9:9, 10, NKJV

Worry

"Peace I leave with you; My peace I give to you; not as the world gives do I give to you. Do not let your heart be troubled, nor let it be fearful."

JOHN 14:27, NASB

Cast all your anxiety on him because he cares for you.

1 PETER 5:7, NIV

"Let not your heart be troubled; you believe in God, believe also in Me."

JOHN 14:1, NKJV

Be anxious for nothing, but in everything by prayer and supplication with thanksgiving let your requests be made known to God. And the peace of God, which surpasses all comprehension, will guard your hearts and your minds in Christ Jesus.

PHILIPPIANS 4:6, 7, NASB

Let the peace of Christ rule in your hearts, to which indeed you were called in one body; and be thankful.

COLOSSIANS 3:15, NASB

And my God will supply all your needs according to His riches in glory in Christ Jesus.

PHILIPPIANS 4:19, NASB

"Therefore I say to you, do not worry about your life, what you will eat or what you will drink; nor about your body, what you will put on. Is not life more than food and the body more than clothing? Look at the birds of the air, for they neither sow nor reap nor gather into barns; yet your heavenly Father feeds them. Are you not of more value than they? Which of you by worrying can add one cubit to his stature? So why do you worry about clothing? Consider the lilies of the field, how they grow: they neither toil nor spin; and yet I say to you that even Solomon in all his glory was not arrayed like one of these. Now if God so clothes the grass of the field, which today is, and tomorrow is thrown into the oven, will He not much more clothe you, O you of little faith? Therefore do not worry, saying, 'What shall we eat?' or 'What shall we drink?' or 'What shall we wear?' For after all these things the Gentiles seek. For your heavenly Father knows that you need all these things. But seek first the kingdom of God and His righteousness, and all these things shall be added to you. Therefore do not worry about tomorrow, for tomorrow will worry about its own things. Sufficient for the day is its own trouble."

MATTHEW 6:25-34, NKJV

The mind of sinful man is death, but the mind controlled by the Spirit is life and peace.

ROMANS 8:6, NIV

For only we who believe can enter his rest. As for the others, God said, "In my anger I took an oath: 'They will never enter my place of rest,'" even though this rest has been ready since he made the world. So there is a special rest still waiting for the people of God.

HEBREWS 4:3, 9, NLT

Those who love Your law have great peace, and nothing causes them to stumble.

PSALM 119:165, NASB

He who dwells in the secret place of the Most High shall abide under the shadow of the Almighty. I will say of the Lord, "He is my refuge and my fortress; My God, in Him I will trust."

PSALM 91:1, 2, NKJV

I fall asleep in peace the moment I lie down because you alone, O Lord, enable me to live securely.

PSALM 4:8, GOD'S WORD

When you lie down, you will not be afraid; when you lie down, your sleep will be sweet.

PROVERBS 3:24, NASB

You will keep in perfect peace all who trust in you, all whose thoughts are fixed on you!

ISAIAH 26:3, NLT

Section 6

The Living Word for Living Life When You Feel Vulnerable or Alone

Loneliness

Singleness

Security

Protection

Loneliness

"For the Lord your God is a compassionate God; He will not fail you nor destroy you nor forget the covenant with your fathers which He swore to them."

DEUTERONOMY 4:31, NASB

"So be strong and courageous! Do not be afraid and do not panic before them. For the Lord your God will personally go ahead of you. He will neither fail you nor abandon you."

DEUTERONOMY 31:6, NLT

"The eternal God is your refuge, and his everlasting arms are under you. He drives out the enemy before you; he cries out, 'Destroy them!'"

DEUTERONOMY 33:27, NLT

"The Lord will not abandon his people, because that would dishonor his great name."

1 SAMUEL 12:22, NLT

Even if my father and mother abandon me, the Lord will take care of me.

PSALM 27:10, GOD'S WORD

God is our refuge and strength, a very present help in trouble.

PSALM 46:1, KJV

He heals the brokenhearted and bandages their wounds.

PSALM 147:3, NLT

"Don't be afraid, because I am with you. Don't be intimidated; I am your God. I will strengthen you. I will help you. I will support you with my victorious right hand."

ISAIAH 41:10, GOD'S WORD

For the mountains may move and the hills disappear, but even then my faithful love for you will remain. My covenant of blessing will never be broken," says the Lord, who has mercy on you.

ISAIAH 54:10, NLT

"Teach these new disciples to obey all the commands I have given you. And be sure of this: I am with you always, even to the end of the age."

MATTHEW 28:20, NLT

"Let not your heart be troubled; you believe in God, believe also in Me."

JOHN 14:1, NKJV

I will not leave you comfortless: I will come to you.

JOHN 14:18, KJV

Do you think anyone is going to be able to drive a wedge between us and Christ's love for us? There is no way! Not trouble, not hard times, not hatred, not hunger, not homelessness, not bullying threats, not backstabbing, not even the worst sins listed in Scripture: "They kill us in cold blood because they hate you. We're sitting ducks; they pick us off one by one." None of this fazes us because Jesus loves us. I'm absolutely convinced that nothing—nothing living or dead, angelic or demonic, today or tomorrow, high or low, thinkable or unthinkable—absolutely *nothing* can get between us and God's love because of the way that Jesus our Master has embraced us.

ROMANS 8:35-39, MSG

Make sure that your character is free from the love of money, being content with what you have; for He Himself has said, "I will never desert you, nor will I ever forsake you."

HEBREWS 13:5, NASB

Cast all your anxiety on him because he cares for you.

1 PETER 5:7, NIV

Singleness

And I will betroth you to Me forever; yes, I will betroth you to Me in righteousness and justice, in steadfast love, and in mercy.

HOSEA 2:19, AMP

Now to the unmarried and widows I say: It is good for them to stay unmarried, as I am.

1 CORINTHIANS 7:8, NIV

Nevertheless, each one should retain the place in life that the Lord assigned to him and to which God has called him. This is the rule I lay down in all the churches.

1 CORINTHIANS 7:17, NIV

Are you married? Do not seek a divorce. Are you unmarried? Do not look for a wife. But if you do marry, you have not sinned; and if a virgin marries, she has not sinned. But those who marry will face many troubles in this life, and I want to spare you this.

1 CORINTHIANS 7:27, 28, NIV

I want you to live as free of complications as possible. When you're unmarried, you're free to concentrate on simply pleasing the Master. Marriage involves you in all the nuts and bolts of domestic life and in wanting to please your spouse, leading to so many more demands on your attention. The time and energy that married people spend on caring for and nurturing each other, the unmarried can spend in becoming whole and holy instruments of God. I'm trying to be helpful and make it as easy as possible for you, not make things harder. All I want is for you to be able to develop a way of life in which you can spend plenty of time together with the Master without a lot of distractions.

1 Corinthians 7:32-35, msg

But the man who has settled the matter in his own mind, who is under no compulsion but has control over his own will, and who has made up his mind not to marry the virgin—this man also does the right thing, So then, he who marries the virgin does right, but he who does not marry her does even better.

1 Corinthians 7:37, 38, niv

Marriage should be honored by all, and the marriage bed kept pure, for God will judge the adulterer and all the sexually immoral.

Hebrews 13:4, niv

Trust in the Lord with all your heart; do not depend on your own understanding. Seek his will in all you do, and he will show you which path to take.

Proverbs 3:5, 6, nlt

Delight yourself in the Lord; and He will give you the desires of your heart.

Psalm 37:4, nasb

Therefore, my brethren, you also have become dead to the law through the body of Christ, that you may be married to another—to Him who was raised from the dead, that we should bear fruit to God.

ROMANS 7:4, NKJV

Each of you must examine your own actions. Then you can be proud of your own accomplishments without comparing yourself to others.

GALATIANS 6:4, GOD'S WORD

For this very reason, make every effort to add to your faith goodness; and to goodness, knowledge; and to knowledge, self-control; and to self-control, perseverance; and to perseverance, godliness; and to godliness, brotherly kindness; and to brotherly kindness, love. For if you possess these qualities in increasing measure, they will keep you from being ineffective and unproductive in your knowledge of our Lord Jesus Christ.

2 PETER 1:5-8, NIV

Let us hold unswervingly to the hope we profess, for he who promised is faithful.

HEBREWS 10:23, NIV

I will not leave you comfortless: I will come to you.

JOHN 14:18, KJV

"Let not your heart be troubled; you believe in God, believe also in Me."

JOHN 14:1, NKJV

He heals the brokenhearted and bandages their wounds.

PSALM 147:3, NLT

God is our refuge and strength, a very present help in trouble.

PSALM 46:1, KJV

Cast all your anxiety on him because he cares for you.

1 PETER 5:7, NIV

But those who hope in the Lord will renew their strength. They will soar on wings like eagles; they will run and not grow weary, they will walk and not be faint.

ISAIAH 40:31, NIV

Be strong and let your heart take courage, all you who hope in the Lord.

PSALM 31:24, NASB

_____

Security

What a God we have! And how fortunate we are to have him, this Father of our Master Jesus! Because Jesus was raised from the dead, we've been given a brand-new life and have everything to live for, including a future in heaven—and the future starts now! God is keeping careful watch over us and the future. The Day is coming when you'll have it all—life healed and whole.

1 PETER 1:3-5, MSG

"My sheep listen to my voice; I know them, and they follow me. I give them eternal life, and they will never perish. No one can snatch them away from me, for my Father has given them to me, and he is more powerful than anyone else. No one can snatch them from the Father's hand."

JOHN 10:27-29, NLT

I'm absolutely convinced that nothing—nothing living or dead, angelic or demonic, today or tomorrow, high or low, thinkable or unthinkable—absolutely *nothing* can get between us and God's love because of the way that Jesus our Master has embraced us.

ROMANS 8:38, 39, MSG

And I am convinced and sure of this very thing, that He Who began a good work in you will continue until the day of Jesus Christ [right up to the time of His return], developing [that good work] and perfecting and bringing it to full completion in you.

PHILIPPIANS 1:6, AMP

But the Lord is faithful, who will establish you and guard you from the evil one.

2 THESSALONIANS 3:3, NKJV

And now to him who can keep you on your feet, standing tall in his bright presence, fresh and celebrating— to our one God, our only Savior, through Jesus Christ, our Master, be glory, majesty, strength, and rule before all time, and now, and to the end of all time. Yes.

JUDE 24, 25, MSG

Lift your eyes and look to the heavens: Who created all these? He who brings out the starry host one by one, and calls them each by name. Because of his great power and strength, not one of them is missing.

ISAIAH 40:26, NIV

Surely goodness and love will follow me all the days of my life, and I will dwell in the house of the Lord forever.

PSALM 23:6, NIV

"But don't be so concerned about perishable things like food. Spend your energy seeking the eternal life that the Son of Man can give you. For God the Father has given me the seal of his approval."

JOHN 6:27, NLT

In addition, he has put his seal of ownership on us and has given us the Spirit as his guarantee.

2 CORINTHIANS 1:22, GOD'S WORD

And now you Gentiles have also heard the truth, the Good News that God saves you. And when you believed in Christ, he identified you as his own by giving you the Holy Spirit, whom he promised long ago.

EPHESIANS 1:13, NLT

Do not grieve the Holy Spirit of God, by whom you were sealed for the day of redemption.

EPHESIANS 4:30, NASB

Our great desire is that you will keep on loving others as long as life lasts, in order to make certain that what you hope for will come true. Then you will not become spiritually dull and indifferent. Instead, you will follow the example of those who are going to inherit God's promises because of their faith and endurance.

HEBREWS 6:11, 12, NLT

So God has given both his promise and his oath. These two things are unchangeable because it is impossible for God to lie. Therefore, we who have fled to him for refuge can have great confidence as we hold to the hope that lies before us. This hope is a strong and trustworthy anchor for our souls. It leads us through the curtain into God's inner sanctuary. Jesus has already gone in there for us. He has become our eternal High Priest in the order of Melchizedek.

HEBREWS 6:18-20, NLT

Protection

The name of the Lord is a strong tower; the [consistently] righteous man [upright and in right standing with God] runs into it and is safe, high [above evil] and strong.

PROVERBS 18:10, AMP

But now, this is what the Lord says—he who created you, O Jacob, he who formed you, O Israel: "Fear not, for I have redeemed you; I have summoned you by name; you are mine. When you pass through the waters, I will be with you; and when you pass through the rivers, they will not sweep over you. When you walk through the fire, you will not be burned; the flames will not set you ablaze.

ISAIAH 43:1, 2, NIV

But the Lord is faithful, and He will strengthen and protect you from the evil one.

2 THESSALONIANS 3:3, NASB

Now who is there to hurt you if you are zealous followers of that which is good?

1 PETER 3:13, AMP

God guards you from every evil, he guards your very life. He guards you when you leave and when you return, he guards you now, he guards you always.

PSALM 121:7, 8, MSG

The Lord is my Light and my Salvation—whom shall I fear or dread? The Lord is the Refuge and Stronghold of my life—of whom shall I be afraid?

PSALM 27:1, AMP

When you lie down, you will not be afraid; when you lie down, your sleep will be sweet.

PROVERBS 3:24, NASB

You have been my refuge, a tower of strength against the enemy.

PSALM 61:3, GOD'S WORD

But whoever listens to me will live in safety and be at ease, without fear of harm.

PROVERBS 1:33, NIV

He is not afraid of bad news. His heart remains secure, full of confidence in the Lord.

PSALM 112:7, GOD'S WORD

If you make the Most High your dwelling—even the Lord, who is my refuge—then no harm will befall you, no disaster will come near your tent.

PSALM 91:9, 10, NIV

I fall asleep in peace the moment I lie down because you alone, O Lord, enable me to live securely.

PSALM 4:8, GOD'S WORD

"You will feel confident because there's hope, and you will look around and rest in safety. You will lie down with no one to frighten you, and many people will try to gain your favor."

JOB 11:18, 19, GOD'S WORD

The beloved of the Lord shall dwell in safety by him; and the Lord shall cover him all the day long, and he shall dwell between his shoulders.

DEUTERONOMY 33:12, KJV

They will no longer be prey for other nations, and wild animals will no longer devour them. They will live in safety, and no one will frighten them.

EZEKIEL 34:28, NLT

"But if you truly obey his voice and do all that I say, then I will be an enemy to your enemies and an adversary to your adversaries."

EXODUS 23:22, NASB

But you, O Lord, will be exalted forever. Your enemies, Lord, will surely perish; all evildoers will be scattered.

PSALM 92:8, 9, NLT

Section 7

The Living Word for Living Life with God

Salvation

God's Correction and Discipline

Freedom from Condemnation

Freedom from Guilt

Salvation

Jesus replied, "I tell you the truth, unless you are born again, you cannot see the Kingdom of God." "What do you mean?" exclaimed Nicodemus. "How can an old man go back into his mother's womb and be born again?" Jesus replied, "I assure you, no one can enter the Kingdom of God without being born of water and the Spirit. Humans can reproduce only human life, but the Holy Spirit gives birth to spiritual life. So don't be surprised when I say, 'You must be born again.'"

JOHN 3:3-7, NLT

This means that anyone who belongs to Christ has become a new person. The old life is gone; a new life has begun!

2 CORINTHIANS 5:17, NLT

For He made Him who knew no sin *to be* sin for us, that we might become the righteousness of God in Him.

2 CORINTHIANS 5:21, NKJV

And you He made alive, who were dead in trespasses and sins.

EPHESIANS 2:1, NKJV

This is good and pleases God our Savior, who wants everyone to be saved and to understand the truth.

1 TIMOTHY 2:3, 4, NLT

My dear children, I write this to you so that you will not sin. But if anybody does sin, we have one who speaks to the Father in our defense—Jesus Christ, the Righteous One. He is the atoning sacrifice for our sins, and not only for ours but also for the sins of the whole world.

1 JOHN 2:1, 2, NIV

You were dead because of your sins and because your sinful nature was not yet cut away. Then God made you alive with Christ, for he forgave all our sins.

COLOSSIANS 2:13, NLT

This is a trustworthy saying that deserves full acceptance (and for this we labor and strive), that we have put our hope in the living God, who is the Savior of all men, and especially of those who believe.

1 TIMOTHY 4:9, 10, NIV

But there is a great difference between Adam's sin and God's gracious gift. For the sin of this one man, Adam, brought death to many. But even greater is God's wonderful grace and his gift of forgiveness to many through this other man, Jesus Christ.

ROMANS 5:15, NLT

But when the kindness and the love of God our Savior toward man appeared, not by works of righteousness which we have done, but according to His mercy He saved us, through the washing of regeneration and renewing of the Holy Spirit, whom He poured out on us abundantly through Jesus Christ our Savior.

TITUS 3:4-6, NKJV

God's Correction and Discipline

Do not reject the discipline of the Lord, my son, and do not resent his warning, because the Lord warns the one he loves, even as a father warns a son with whom he is pleased.

PROVERBS 3:11, 12, GOD'S WORD

"So, what a blessing when God steps in and corrects you! Mind you, don't despise the discipline of Almighty God! True, he wounds, but he also dresses the wound; the same hand that hurts you, heals you."

JOB 5:17, 18, MSG

Blessed is the man you discipline, O Lord; the man you teach from your law; you grant him relief from days of trouble, till a pit is dug for the wicked.

PSALM 94:12, 13, NIV

But when the Lord judges us, he disciplines us so that we won't be condemned along with the rest of the world.

1 CORINTHIANS 11:32, GOD'S WORD

That is why we never give up. Though our bodies are dying, our spirits are being renewed every day. For our present troubles are small and won't last very long. Yet they produce for us a glory that vastly outweighs them and will last forever!

2 CORINTHIANS 4:16, 17, NLT

So don't feel sorry for yourselves. Or have you forgotten how good parents treat children, and that God regards you as his children? My dear child, don't shrug off God's discipline, but don't be crushed by it either. It's the child he loves that he disciplines; the child he embraces, he also corrects. God is educating you; that's why you must never drop out. He's treating you as dear children. This trouble you're in isn't punishment; it's training, the normal experience of children. Only irresponsible parents leave children to fend for themselves. Would you prefer an irresponsible God? We respect our own parents for training and not spoiling us, so why not embrace God's training so we can truly live? While we were children, our parents did what seemed best to them. But God is doing what is best for us, training us to live God's holy best. At the time, discipline isn't much fun. It always feels like it's going against the grain. Later, of course, it pays off handsomely, for it's the well-trained who find themselves mature in their relationship with God.

HEBREWS 12:5-11, MSG

Freedom from Condemnation

There is therefore now no condemnation to them which are in Christ Jesus, who walk not after the flesh, but after the Spirit.

ROMANS 8:1, KJV

He has not dealt with us according to our sins, nor rewarded us according to our iniquities. As far as the east is from the west, so far has He removed our transgressions from us.

PSALM 103:10, 12, NASB

This means that anyone who belongs to Christ has become a new person. The old life is gone; a new life has begun!

2 CORINTHIANS 5:17, NLT

"For God did not send His Son into the world to condemn the world, but that the world through Him might be saved."

JOHN 3:17, NKJV

"I tell you the truth, whoever hears my word and believes him who sent me has eternal life and will not be condemned; he has crossed over from death to life."

JOHN 5:24, NIV

For I will be merciful to their unrighteousness, and their sins and their iniquities will I remember no more.

HEBREWS, 8:12, KJV

I, even I, am He who blots out your transgressions for My own sake; and I will not remember your sins.

ISAIAH 43:25, NKJV

Let wicked people abandon their ways. Let evil people abandon their thoughts. Let them return to the Lord, and he will show compassion to them. Let them return to our God, because he will freely forgive them.

ISAIAH 55:7, GOD'S WORD

I acknowledged my sin to You, and my iniquity I did not hide. I said, I will confess my transgressions to the Lord [continually unfolding the past till all is told]—then You [instantly] forgave me the guilt and iniquity of my sin.

PSALM 32:5, AMP

If we confess our sins, he is faithful and just to forgive us our sins, and to cleanse us from all unrighteousness.

1 JOHN 1:9, KJV

Blessed is he whose transgression is forgiven, whose sin is covered.

PSALM 32:1, KJV

"Then I heard a loud voice shouting across the heavens, "It has come at last—salvation and power and the Kingdom of our God, and the authority of his Christ. For the accuser of our brothers and sisters has been thrown down to earth—the one who accuses them before our God day and night. And they have defeated him by the blood of the Lamb and by their testimony. And they did not love their lives so much that they were afraid to die."

REVELATION 12:10, 11, NLT

Jesus straightened up and asked her, "Woman, where are they? Has no one condemned you?" "No one, sir," she said. "Then neither do I condemn you," Jesus declared. "Go now and leave your life of sin."

JOHN 8:10, 11, NIV

"And they will not need to teach their neighbors, nor will they need to teach their relatives, saying, 'You should know the Lord.' For everyone, from the least to the greatest, will know me already," says the Lord. "And I will forgive their wickedness, and I will never again remember their sins."

JEREMIAH 31:34, NLT

Let us draw near with a true heart in full assurance of faith, having our hearts sprinkled from an evil conscience, and our bodies washed with pure water.

HEBREWS 10:22, KJV

"When you return to the Lord, your relatives and children will find compassion from those who captured them. They will return to this land. The Lord your

God is merciful and compassionate. He will not turn his face away from you if you return to him."

2 CHRONICLES 30:9, GOD'S WORD

———————

Freedom from Guilt

Let the wicked forsake his way, and the unrighteous man his thoughts: and let him return unto the Lord, and he will have mercy upon him; and to our God, for he will abundantly pardon.

ISAIAH 55:7, KJV

"When you return to the Lord, your relatives and children will find compassion from those who captured them. They will return to this land. The Lord your God is merciful and compassionate. He will not turn his face away from you if you return to him."

2 CHRONICLES 30:9, GOD'S WORD

Even if we feel guilty, God is greater than our feelings, and he knows everything.

1 JOHN 3:20, NLT

"And they will not need to teach their neighbors, nor will they need to teach their relatives, saying, 'You should know the Lord.' For everyone, from the least to the greatest, will know me already," says the Lord. "And I will forgive their wickedness, and I will never again remember their sins."

JEREMIAH 31:34, NLT

I am writing to you, little children, because your sins have been forgiven you for His name's sake.

1 JOHN 2:12, NASB

"I, even I, am He who blots out your transgressions for My own sake; and I will not remember your sins."

ISAIAH 43:25, NKJV

But if we walk in the Light as He Himself is in the Light, we have fellowship with one another, and the blood of Jesus His Son cleanses us from all sin.

1 JOHN 1:7, NASB

Section 8

The Living Word for Living Life When You Want to Celebrate

Joy
Praise

Joy

Happy are those who hear the joyful call to worship, for they will walk in the light of your presence, Lord.

PSALM 89:15, 16, NLT

You have filled my heart with greater joy than when their grain and new wine abound.

PSALM 4:7, NIV

"You will go out in joy and be led forth in peace; the mountains and hills will burst into song before you, and all the trees of the field will clap their hands."

ISAIAH 55:12, NIV

Shouts of joy and victory resound in the tents of the righteous: "The Lord's right hand has done mighty things!"

PSALM 118:15, NIV

Those who sow in tears Shall reap in joy. He who continually goes forth weeping, bearing seed for sowing, Shall doubtless come again with rejoicing, bringing his sheaves with him.

PSALM 126:5, 6, NKJV

Light is sown like seed for the righteous and gladness for the upright in heart. Be glad in the Lord, you righteous ones, and give thanks to His holy name.

PSALM 97:11, 12, NASB

You'll take delight in God, the Mighty One, and look to him joyfully, boldly.

JOB 22:26, MSG

These things have I spoken unto you, that my joy might remain in you, and that your joy might be full.

JOHN 15:11, KJV

Yet I will rejoice in the Lord, I will joy in the God of my salvation.

HABAKKUK 3:18, KJV

[The Lord God says] And the redeemed of the Lord shall return and come with singing to Zion; everlasting joy shall be upon their heads. They shall obtain joy and gladness, and sorrow and sighing shall flee away.

ISAIAH 51:11, AMP

For our heart shall rejoice in him, because we have trusted in his holy name.

PSALM 33:21, KJV

Though you have not seen him, you love him; and even though you do not see him now, you believe in him and are filled with an inexpressible and glorious joy.

1 PETER 1:8, NIV

And Nehemiah continued, "Go and celebrate with a feast of rich foods and sweet drinks, and share gifts of food with people who have nothing prepared. This is a sacred day before our Lord. Don't be dejected and sad, for the joy of the Lord is your strength!"

NEHEMIAH 8:10, NLT

I am overwhelmed with joy in the Lord my God! For he has dressed me with the clothing of salvation and draped me in a robe of righteousness. I am like a bridegroom in his wedding suit or a bride with her jewels.

ISAIAH 61:10, NLT

Let the righteous rejoice in the Lord and take refuge in him; let all the upright in heart praise him!

PSALM 64:10, NIV

You satisfy my soul with the richest foods. My mouth will sing your praise with joyful lips.

PSALM 63:5, GOD'S WORD

But let the righteous be glad; let them exult before God; yes, let them rejoice with gladness.

PSALM 68:3, NASB

"Therefore you too have grief now; but I will see you again, and your heart will rejoice, and no one will take your joy away from you."

JOHN 16:22, NASB

———————

Praise

I will bless the Lord at all times: his praise shall continually be in my mouth.

PSALM 34:1, KJV

I will also praise You with a harp, even Your truth, O my God; to You I will sing praises with the lyre, O Holy One of Israel. My lips will shout for joy when I sing praises to You; and my soul, which You have redeemed.

PSALM 71:22, 23, NASB

Make a joyful shout to the Lord, all you lands! Serve the Lord with gladness; come before His presence with singing. Know that the Lord, He is God; it is He who has made us, and not we ourselves; we are His people and the sheep of His pasture. Enter into His gates with thanksgiving, and into His courts with praise. Be thankful to Him, and bless His name. For the Lord is good; His mercy is everlasting, and His truth endures to all generations.

PSALM 100:1-5, NKJV

Bless the Lord, O my soul; and all that is within me, bless His holy name! Bless the Lord, O my soul, and forget not all His benefits: who forgives all your iniquities, who heals all your diseases, who redeems your life from destruction, who crowns you with lovingkindness and tender mercies, who satisfies your mouth with good things, So that your youth is renewed like the eagle's.

PSALM 103:1-5, NKJV

Bless the Lord, you His angels, who excel in strength, who do His word, heeding the voice of His word. Bless the Lord, all you His hosts, you ministers of His, who do His pleasure. Bless the Lord, all His works, in all places of His dominion. Bless the Lord, O my soul!

PSALM 103:20-22, NKJV

Praise the Lord! Yes, give praise, O servants of the Lord. Praise the name of the Lord! Blessed be the name of the Lord now and forever. Everywhere— from east to west—praise the name of the Lord. For the Lord is high above the nations; his glory is higher than the heavens.

PSALM 113:1-4, NLT

I lift you high in praise, my God, O my King! and I'll bless your name into eternity. I'll bless you every day, and keep it up from now to eternity. God is magnificent; he can never be praised enough. There are no boundaries to his greatness. Generation after generation stands in awe of your work; each one tells stories of your mighty acts. Your beauty and splendor have everyone talking; I compose songs on your wonders. Your marvelous doings are headline news; I could write a book full of the details of your greatness. The fame of your goodness spreads across the country; your righteousness is on everyone's lips.

PSALM 145:1-7, MSG

Praise the Lord! Praise the Lord from the heavens; praise Him in the heights! Praise Him, all His angels; praise Him, all His hosts! Praise Him, sun and moon; Praise Him, all stars of light! Praise Him, highest heavens, and the waters that are above the heavens. Let them praise the name of the Lord, for He commanded and they were created.

PSALM 148:1-5, NASB

Blessed be the God and Father of our Lord Jesus Christ, who has blessed us with every spiritual blessing in the heavenly places in Christ.

EPHESIANS 1:3, NASB

Through Jesus, therefore, let us continually offer to God a sacrifice of praise—the fruit of lips that confess his name.

HEBREWS 13:15, NIV

Is anyone among you suffering? Then he must pray. Is anyone cheerful? He is to sing praises.

JAMES 5:13, NASB

Saying with a loud voice, Worthy is the Lamb that was slain to receive power, and riches, and wisdom, and strength, and honour, and glory, and blessing.

REVELATION 5:12, KJV

Saying, Amen: Blessing, and glory, and wisdom, and thanksgiving, and honour, and power, and might, be unto our God for ever and ever. Amen.

REVELATION 7:12, KJV

Then I heard again what sounded like the shout of a vast crowd or the roar of mighty ocean waves or the crash of loud thunder: "Praise the Lord! For the Lord our God, the Almighty, reigns. Let us be glad and rejoice, and let us give honor to him. For the time has come for the wedding feast of the Lamb, and his bride has prepared herself."

REVELATION 19:6, 7, NLT

And again, "Praise the Lord, all you Gentiles, and sing praises to him, all you peoples."

ROMANS 15:11, NIV

Summing it all up, friends, I'd say you'll do best by filling your minds and meditating on things true, noble, reputable, authentic, compelling, gracious—the best, not the worst; the beautiful, not the ugly; things to praise, not things to curse.

PHILIPPIANS 4:8, MSG

The purpose of these troubles is to test your faith as fire tests how genuine gold is. Your faith is more precious than gold, and by passing the test, it gives praise, glory, and honor to God. This will happen when Jesus Christ appears again.

1 PETER 1:7, GOD'S WORD

For it is written: "As I live, says the Lord, every knee shall bow to Me, and every tongue shall confess to God."

ROMANS 14:11, NKJV

Prayer For Salvation

*H*eavenly Father, You said in Your Word that whoever shall call upon the name of the Lord shall be saved, so I am calling on Jesus right now. Lord Jesus, I believe You died on the Cross for my sins, and that You were raised from the dead. I ask You to come into my heart. Take control of my life and help me be what You want me to be. I repent of my sins and surrender myself totally and completely to You. I accept You and confess You as my Lord and Savior. Thank You, Father, for forgiving me, adopting me as Your child, and making me a new person. In Jesus' name I pray, amen.

Welcome to God's family!

•••

If you prayed this prayer to receive Jesus Christ as your Savior for the first time, please contact us on the web at *www.theworshipcentercc.org*

Or, write to us at V. H. Moody Ministries | 100 Derby Parkway | Birmingham, AL 35215

Where to Find It

Addiction: Addiction, Temptation, Freedom from Condemnation, Freedom from Guilt

Aloneness: Grief, Loneliness, Singleness

Anger: Anger, Contentment, Peace

Anxiety: Contentment, Overcoming Difficulty, Peace, Security, Stress, Worry

Bad Habits: Addiction, Temptation, Freedom from Condemnation, Freedom from Guilt

Bad News: God's Provision, Overcoming Difficulty, Peace, Strength, Sickness, Suffering

Betrayal: Enemies

Bondage: Addiction

Budget: Money, Wisdom

Business: Business, Success, Wisdom

Breakthrough: Addiction, Overcoming Difficulty, Strength, Waiting on God

Career: Business, Success

Celebration: Joy, Praise

Challenges: Overcoming Difficulty, Stress, Wisdom

Children: Children, Family, Relationships

Comparison with Others: Envy

Competition: Envy

Condemnation: Freedom from Condemnation, Addiction, Freedom from Guilt, Salvation, Temptation

Confusion: Wisdom

Contentment: Contentment, Peace, Anger

Death: Grief, Loneliness, God's Provision, Singleness

Debt: Money, Wisdom, God's Provision

Decisions: Wisdom

Destiny: Purpose

Depression: Depression, Grief, Loneliness, Overcoming Difficulty, Suffering

Difficulty: Overcoming Difficulty, Stress, Strength, Suffering

Disappointment: God's Provision, Overcoming Difficulty, Waiting on God

Discouragement: Overcoming Difficulty

Divorce: Loneliness, God's Provision, Overcoming Difficulty, Stress, Singleness, Wisdom

Emotions: Anger, Depression, Envy, Grief, Joy, Peace, Worry

Enemies: Enemies

Envy: Envy

Eternal Life: Salvation

Expectant Parents: Children, Family, Marriage

Faith: Freedom from Condemnation, Freedom from Guilt, God's Provision, Overcoming Difficulty, Purpose, Salvation, Sickness, Suffering

Family: Family, Children, Marriage

Fear: Peace, Protection, Security, Worry

Fear of the Future: God's Provision, Peace, Purpose,

Salvation

Finances: God's Provision, Money

Forgiveness: Freedom from Condemnation, Freedom from Guilt, Salvation

Guilt: Freedom from Guilt, Addiction, Freedom from Condemnation, Salvation, Sin, Temptation

Frustration: Anger, Contentment, Peace, Waiting on God

God's Correction: God's Correction and Discipline, Temptation

God's Discipline: God's Correction and Discipline

God's Provision: God's Provision, Money, Overcoming Difficulty, Stress, Waiting on God

God's Timing: Waiting on God

Grief: Grief, Depression, Loneliness, Singleness

Happiness: Joy, Praise

Health and Healing: Sickness

Heaviness: Depression, Suffering

Hope: Addiction, Depression, Grief, Loneliness, Purpose, Salvation, Sickness, Suffering

Home Life: Children, Family, Marriage

Insecurity: Security

Jealousy: Envy

Job: Business

Job Loss: God's Provision, Waiting on God, Wisdom

Joy: Joy, Praise

Living in Freedom: Addiction, Freedom from Condemnation, Freedom from Guilt

Loneliness: Loneliness, Depression, Grief, Singleness, Suffering

Loss: Grief, Suffering, God's Provision

Love: Children, Family, Marriage

Love of God: Freedom from Condemnation, Freedom from Guilt, God's Correction and Discipline, Loneliness, Peace, Protection, Security, Suffering

Marriage: Marriage, Family, Singleness

Money: Money, God's Provision, Success, Wisdom

Need: God's Provision, Waiting on God

Needing Direction: Purpose, Waiting on God, Wisdom

Obedience: God's Correction and Discipline, Temptation, Waiting on God

Offense: Enemies

Parenting: Children, Family

Patience: Waiting on God

Peace: Peace, Anger, Contentment, Protection, Security, Stress, Salvation, Worry

Perseverance: Overcoming Difficulty, Suffering

Praise: Praise, Joy

Professional Life: Business

Protection: Protection, Peace, Salvation, Security

Purpose: Purpose

Rage: Anger, Peace

Regret: Freedom from Condemnation, Freedom from Guilt

Relationship with God: Freedom from Condemnation,

Freedom from Guilt, God's Correction and Discipline, Salvation, Waiting on God

Relationships: Children, Enemies, Envy, Family, Marriage

Repentance: Freedom from Condemnation, Freedom from Guilt, Salvation

Resources: God's Provision, Money

Revenge: Anger

Raising Teenagers: Children, Family

Sadness: Depression, Grief, Loneliness

Salvation: Salvation, Freedom from Condemnation, Freedom from Guilt, Peace, Protection, Security

Satisfaction: Contentment, Peace

Security: Security, Peace, Protection, Salvation

Sickness: Sickness, Suffering

Sin: Freedom from Condemnation, Freedom from Guilt, Salvation

Single Parents: Children, Family, Loneliness, Singleness

Singleness: Singleness, God's Provision, Loneliness, Waiting on God

Stewardship: Money

Strength: Strength, Overcoming Difficulty, Suffering

Stress: Stress, God's Provision, Overcoming Difficulty, Peace, Worry

Success: Success, Business, Money, Wisdom

Suffering: Suffering, Overcoming Difficulty, Sickness, Strength

Temptation: Temptation, Addiction, Freedom from

Condemnation, Freedom from Guilt, God's Correction and Discipline, Strength

Trusting God: God's Provision, Waiting on God

Waiting on God: Waiting on God

Weariness: Strength

Wisdom: Wisdom, Business, Money, Success,

Work: Business

Worship: Praise

Worry: Worry, Overcoming Difficulty, Peace, Stress

About Van Moody

*V*an Moody has a passion for healthy transformation in individuals, organizations and the world. With a background in business, marketing and ministry he is uniquely qualified to position and empower people for genuine success in every area of life.

A native of Atlanta, Georgia, Moody has studied at some of the most respected institutions in the world. His voice has been heard around the world: at the 30th Anniversary of the March on Washington, with Pope John Paul II and his Pontifical Council in Rome, Italy; as an Associate Trainer for Dr. John Maxwell's leadership organization, EQUIP, in Tokyo, Japan; and most recently, as a member of Dr. Oz's Core Team featured on the Dr. Oz Show on ABC. Moody also established a thriving ministry, The Worship Center Christian Church, which has two Alabama locations as well as an online campus, which serves thousands weekly.

With his unique ability to understand and communicate timeless truths in highly relevant, contemporary ways, Moody challenges and equips the world to fulfill their potential and live their purpose. Known for his keen insights and practical application, Moody is a strong visionary leader, and a sought-after speaker and leader in both the church and business communities.

Moody is the author of the best-selling book, *The People Factor* (Thomas Nelson), and *The I –Factor* (Thomas Nelson) and resides in Birmingham, Alabama with his wife, Dr. Ty, and their two children, Eden Sydney and Ethan Isaiah.

Other Books by Van Moody

The I Factor: How Building a Great Relationship with Yourself Is the Key to a Happy, Successful Life

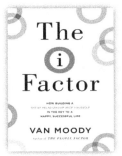

One question lies behind every struggle we face: How do I deal with myself?

Behind all our stumbles, behind each of our missteps, behind every one of our failings lies an inability to handle what Van Moody calls the "I-Factor."

More than self-worth or self-respect, beyond even character and perception of purpose, the I-Factor is about managing yourself—your whole life—well. In his inspiring new book, Moody reveals how to get hold of your I-Factor.

Moody identifies three dynamics essential to winning the battle of the I-Factor: identity, significance, and perspective. When you understand your identity you know who you are, setting your foundation for everything.

When you understand your significance, you see the purpose and the greatness you were created for. And when you understand perspective, you can view the problems you face as stepping-stones to greatness rather than stumbling blocks. Properly understand these three dynamics, and you will be able to master your I-Factor.

Weaving together personal stories, practical principles, and profound biblical truth, The I-Factor provides the key to achieving the life of greatness that you are destined for.

The I Factor: 8-Week Small Group Study Guide

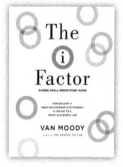

The key to the life you want is inside you.

One question lies behind every struggle we face: How do I deal with myself? Behind all our stumbles, behind each of our missteps, behind every one of our failings lies an inability to handle what Van Moody calls the "I-Factor."

More than self-worth or self-respect, beyond even character and perception of purpose, the I-Factor is about managing yourself-your whole life-well. In this 8-week small group curriculum, you'll learn more about your I-Factor, discover important insights about how it affects your life, and connect with others for further growth.

In this study, Van Moody helps you build a foundation by understanding your identity, seeing the purpose you were created for by understanding your significance, and viewing your problems as stepping stones to greatness by understanding your perspective. With personal stories, practical principles, and profound biblical truth, The I-Factor provides the key to achieving the life of greatness you are destined for.

The People Factor: How Building Great Relationships and Ending Bad Ones Unlocks Your God-Given Purpose

The relationships in your life will make the difference between happiness and misery.

The right relationship will launch you to the heights of achievement; the wrong one will tether you to mediocrity. Your relationships will be your sources of greatest joy and your venues of greatest pain. Van Moody says, "When people show you who they are, pay attention."

We need to undertake the important task of evaluating our relation-

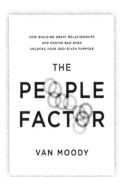

ships intelligently. We need to recognize the people with whom God has called us to walk in mutually beneficial relationships and to identify those who will derail our destinies or hinder His purposes for our lives. It is high time we cultivate our Relational IQs, understanding not only how to build great relationships but also how to avoid or skillfully exit bad ones.

Van Moody saw this need every day of his pastoral life, but he could not find a concise, practical resource for people who need to become more relationally savvy. He needed a beyond-the-basics study guide for Relational IQ. The People Factor is his solution.

God works in our lives through our relationships. Yet, all too often, we get our relationship advice from the most toxic sources we can find. The People Factor is based on the most effective, trustworthy relationship book of all time: the Bible.

If you hunger for a richer, more fulfilling life, your Relational IQ is the place to start. If you put The People Factor principles to work, you will become stronger, happier, and healthier in all your relationships. You will be a better spouse, a better friend, a better boss, a better parent, and a better person.